DEATH WITH DIGNITY:
LEGALIZED PHYSICIAN-ASSISTED DEATH
IN THE UNITED STATES

Oregon Death with Dignity Act
Washington Death with Dignity Act

Stuart C. Goldberg

Library of Congress Cataloging-in-Publication Data.

Goldberg, Stuart C. (Stuart C. Goldberg)
Death with Dignity
Legalized Physician-Assisted Death in the United States

IBSN-10   1463650841
IBSN-13   978-1463650841

1. Goldberg, Stuart C.
2. Stuart C. Goldberg
3. Death with Dignity
4. Assisted Suicide
5. Suicide, Assisted
6. Suicide
7. Physician-Assisted Suicide
8. Physician-Assisted Death
9. Mercy Killing
10. Euthanasia
11. Terminal Illness
12. Terminal Disease
13. Terminal Sedation
14. Qualified Patient
15. Lethal Injection
16. Doctor Death
17. Kevorkian, Jack
18. Oregon Death with Dignity Act
19. Washington Death with Dignity Act
20. Cruzan v. Missouri
21. Washington v. Glucksberg
22. Gonzales v. Oregon
23. Lethal Dose of Medication
24. Right to Die
25. End of Life
26. Good Death
27. Peaceful Death
28. Self-Deliverance

Printed in the United States of America

Stuart C. Goldberg
www.PublicInvestorsAttorney.com

TABLE OF CONTENTS

NOTE: This book does not contain legal or medical advice, which can only be obtained from the reader's personal attorney or physician.

DEDICATIONS

627,980 OREGON VOTERS

To the 627,980 insightful voters who cast their votes in favor of the Oregon Death with Dignity Act on November 8, 1994, thus becoming the first state to legalize physician-assisted death, and creating a template for other states to follow.

1,715,219 WASHINGTON VOTERS

To the 1,715,219 voters who cast their votes in favor of the Washington Death with Dignity Act on November 4, 2008, thus becoming the second state to legalize physician-assisted death.

ACKNOWLEDGMENTS

I own a special debt of gratitude to my neighbors and friends who provided invaluable comments, corrections and suggestions: Gary Friedman, Abe Orlick, Cory Schidler, Frani and Norman Wolfe, and especially to Eddie Katz for his exceptional effort and keen eyes. Lastly, and most importantly, to my first and third wives—the perfect book ends to a most interesting life.

INTRODUCTION
OREGON DEATH WITH DIGNITY ACT-2011
WASHINGTON DEATH WITH DIGNITY ACT-2011

A painless death is one of life's greatest blessings. As expressed by two nineteenth century philosophers and poets:

Darkling I listen; and, for many a time
I have been half in love with easeful death,
Called him soft names in many a mused rhyme,
To take into the air my quiet breath;
Now more than ever seems it rich to die,
To cease upon the midnight with no pain

[John Keats, *Ode to a Nightingale* (1820), st. 6]

Death is as natural as life,
and should be sweet and graceful.

[Ralph Waldo Emerson, 1850]

Those who are fortunate, die in relative peace. The unfortunate, as stated by Supreme Court Justice Stevens, are "torture[d]" to death while being connected to machines that sentence the patient to a "living hell":

Highly invasive treatment may perpetuate human existence through a merger of body and machine that some might reasonably regard as an insult to life, rather than as its continuation.

[Cruzan v. Missouri (Su. Ct. 1990), Stevens dissenting at p. 339]

When the torture becomes excruciating and unbearable, there are some who will seek an act of kindness through physician-assisted death (no longer referred to as physician-assisted suicide).

Traditionally, the primary tension in the area of "physician-assisted suicide" (now referred to as physician-assisted death), has been between, on the one hand: employing medication to alleviate pain even though it "hastens death," (a legally accepted medical practice throughout the United States); and on the other hand, prescribing a lethal dose of medication that "causes death," (a practice historically treated as homicide).

It was not until the adoption of Death with Dignity Acts in the State of Oregon in 1994 and then again in 1997, and the State of Washington in 2008, that prescribing "medication to end [a qualified patient's] life in a humane and dignified manner," was made legal for residents of these two states. As of the beginning of 2011, Oregon and Washington were the only two states with such legislation, but similar laws have been advocated in other states.

In this book, three chapters have been assigned to each state's Death with Dignity Act, describing: 1)-the requirements nessary to become a "qualified patient," 2)-the procedures to be followed, and 3)-the statistics relating to that state's patients (525 in Oregon, and 119 in Washington, making a total of 644). For Oregon residents these three chapters are numbered one, two and three. For Washington residents these three chapters are numbered four, five and six. For resident of all other states, the Oregon chapters are most relevant.

In addition, separate chapters (seven, eight and nine) are devoted to an in-depth analysis of the three most important Supreme Court cases involving the death with dignity controversy: Cruzan v. Missouri (Su. Ct. 1990), Washington v. Glucksberg (Su. Ct.1997), and Gonzales v. Oregon (Su. Ct. 2006).

Appendix-A contains the entire text of the Oregon Death with Dignity Act; and Appendix-B contains the entire text of the Washington Death with Dignity Act.

The Oregon law, upon which the Washington law is modeled, may be considered pure genius. It contains exacting standards as to what constitutes a "qualified patient," and also sets forth numerous safeguards.

In short, a "qualified patient," is: a)-an adult, b)-resident of the state, c)-capable of making a voluntary and informed decision, d)-suffering from a terminal disease, with death predicted to be within six months or less; and, e)-physically able to self-administer the prescribed lethal dose of medication.

The Acts also contain numerous safeguards, such as: a)-limiting availability to only "qualified patients," b)-mandating that the patient make three separate requests, c)-imposed waiting periods, d)-providing rights to rescind at every stage of the process, e)-requiring a second opinion from an independent consulting physician, f)-psychiatric evaluation if serious depression or other mental illness is suspected, and g)-mandating self-administration of the prescribed medication.

The statistics involving Oregon's thirteen years of experience, and Washington's two years of experience, are most revealing and are treated in chapter-3 for Oregon and chapter-6 for Washington. Some interesting facts include: a rather short average physician-patient relationship (10 weeks in Oregon, and between 3-24 weeks for over half the patients in Washington); an overwhelming percentage of the patients coming by way of hospice (Oregon—86%, Washington—79%); a low percentage of patients referred to psychiatric evaluation (Oregon—7%, Washington—4%); low number of prescribing physicians present when medication was taken (Oregon—18%, Washington—6%); a consistently higher degree of those with a college education (Oregon—44% compared to an Oregon state average of 25%; Washington—42% compared to a Washington state average of 31%, and a national average of 28%); a demographic overwhelmingly white; and, the number of physicians involved in the programs in excess of 100.

It is also noteworthy that the leading medical authority in the field recommends that physicians not make the patient initially aware of the existence of the Death with Dignity Acts. It is up to the patient to broach the subject.

By first reading this book, a potential candidate can learn the technicalities of the process in order to meet the requirements of becoming a "qualified patient." For example, a requirement that specifies: "If in the opinion of the attending physician or the consulting physician a patient may be suffering from a psychiatric or psychological disorder or depression causing impaired judgment, either physician shall refer the patient for counseling." Thus, while some degree of sadness is to be expected as a result of a terminal illness, an "unremitting low mood,… despondency, and pervasive low self-esteem are all hallmarks of significant depression." Accordingly, it behooves one trying to become a qualified patient to present a calm, lucid and rational appearance.

The terminology: "suicide," "assisted suicide," "mercy killing," and "homicide," are words specifically forbidden to be used under the Oregon and Washington Death with Dignity Acts. In accordance with the Washington Act: "state reports shall refer to practice under [the Act] as obtaining and self-administering life-ending medication."

Self administration of the medication by the patient is one of the necessities of the Acts. Accordingly, there is nothing in these Acts that "authorizes a physician or any other person to end a patient's life by lethal injection, mercy killing, or active euthanasia."

What if a person has an insurance policy that denies coverage in the event of suicide? The answer is that such a provision is not valid within the context of a patient's ending his/her life under the Death with Dignity Acts.

Immunity from criminal and civil liabilities is also provided to those physicians and other individuals: "for participating in good faith compliance with [the Death with Dignity Acts] when a qualified patient takes the prescribed medication to end his or her life in a humane and dignified manner."

A knowledge of the three principal Supreme Court cases is also important for an understanding of the legal groundwork that led up to the Death with Dignity Acts.

The landmark 1990 Supreme Court decision in <u>Cruzan v. Missouri</u> was, in the words of the Court: "[T]he first case in which we have been squarely presented with the issue of whether the United States Constitution grants what is in common parlance referred to as a 'right to die.'" The holding in this case, as it relates to this question, was that patients have the right to end their lives by refusing or discontinuing "death prolonging procedures" and "life-sustaining medical treatment," such as "artificially-delivered food and water essential to life." In other words, in 1990, a patient had the absolute legal right to chose to starve to death over a period of days or weeks in the plain sight of family and/or hospital staff, but did not have the right to receive a prescription for a lethal dose of medication to end his/her life in a humane manner within minutes or hours.

In <u>Washington v. Glucksberg</u>, a 1997 Supreme Court case, the issue of "physician-assisted suicide" was directly before the Court. The original plaintiffs in this case were: 1)-Dr. Glucksberg and several of his colleagues who "occasionally treat terminally ill, suffering patients, and stated that they would assist these patients in ending their lives if not for Washington's assisted-suicide ban," and 2)-three of their patients. The plaintiffs in <u>Glucksberg</u> succinctly stated the issues as: "Is there a right to die," and a right to "control of one's final days," and described the asserted liberty as "the right to choose a humane, dignified death," and "the liberty to shape death." The Court's answer to these questions, was a resounding "no." The State of Washington's ban on physician-assisted suicide was unanimously upheld. But the Court did look favorably on the Oregon Death with Dignity Act as a valid issue of states rights.

The 2006 Supreme Court of <u>Gonzales v. Oregon</u>, presented a direct challenge to the Oregon Death with Dignity Act. In 1994, and then again in 1997, a voters' referendum in the State of Oregon was decided in favor of adopting the Oregon Death with Dignity Act This statute, for the first time in the history of the United States, permitted physician-assisted death. As would be expected, this Oregon Act was passed over the vigorous opposition of both traditional medical organizations and the pro-life movement. What the opposition could not accomplish at the ballot boxes, Attorney General John Ashcroft attempted to do by a 2001 "Interpretive Rule" which decreed that the prescription of a lethal dose of medication was in violation of the federal Controlled Substance Act. The Supreme Court sustained an injunction against the Attorney General's attempt to overturn the Oregon Death with Dignity Act.

<u>This book was written with four audiences in mind</u>:

- Residents of Oregon and Washington who need to know about their state's Death with Dignity Act.
- Residents of the other 48 states and other jurisdictions who want to know how to adopt similar legislation.
- All those who want to learn about the thirteen years of actual experience in administrating the Oregon Act, and the two years of actual experience in administering the Washington Act. and
- Legislators of states without Death with Dignity Acts who want a template to adopt such legislation.

Stuart C. Goldberg
September, 2011

PART-I
OREGON DEATH WITH DIGNITY ACT

To be read by residents of the state of Oregon and all other jurisdictions except for residents of the state of Washington (for whom Part-II is presented).

CHAPTER-ONE
QUALIFIED PATIENT

OREGON DEATH WITH DIGNITY ACT
("ODWDA") or ("Oregon Act")

TABLE OF CONTENTS

NOTE: This chapter/book does not contain legal or medical advice, which can only be obtained from the reader's personal attorney or physician.

§1.01)-"QUALIFIED PATIENT"

ONLY A "QUALIFIED PATIENT" IS ELIGIBLE TO RECEIVE THE BENEFITS OF THE OREGON DEATH WITH DIGNITY ACT.

The Oregon Death with Dignity Act ("ODWDA") or ("the OREGON ACT") limits it applicability to a "qualified patient":

> **"Qualified patient"** means a capable adult who is a resident of Oregon and has satisfied the requirements of [the ODWDA] in order to obtain a prescription for medication to end his or her life in a humane and dignified manner.
>
> [ODWDA 127.800§1.01(11)]

§1.02)-"ADULT"—18 YEARS OLD OR OLDER

ONLY AN "ADULT," 18 YEARS OLD OR OLDER CAN BE A QUALIFIED PATIENT.

The first requirement to be considered a "qualified patient," is that the patient must be an adult defined as an individual who is eighteen years of age or older. [ODWDA 127.800 §1.01(1)]

In the thirteen year history of the Oregon Act (1998-2010), out of 525 patients there were 6 patients—(1%) in the 18-34 age group, with the youngest being 25.

In the two year history of the Washington Act (2009-2010), out of 119 patients none were in the age groups of 18-34 or 35-44, with the youngest patient being 48.

§1.03)-"RESIDENT" REQUIREMENT

ONLY A "RESIDENT" OF THE STATE OF OREGON CAN BE A QUALIFIED PATIENT.

The second requirement to be considered a "qualified patient," is to be a resident of the State of Oregon:

> **Who may initiate a written request for medication:**
> … a resident of Oregon….
>
> [ODWDA 127.805 §2.01(1)]

A)-OREGON DEFINITION OF RESIDENT: The most common area in which the concept of residency is at issue is in the realm of taxation. If you are a resident of the State of Oregon, you must file an Oregon tax return. According to the Oregon Department of Revenue, the answer to the question posed on their website "Are you a resident?" sets forth three criteria as follows:

> 1)-You think of Oregon as your permanent home.
> 2)-Oregon is the center of your financial, social, and family life.
> 3)-Oregon is the place you intend to come back to when you are away.
>
> [http://www.oregon.gov/DOR/PERTAX/faq-qa_forms.shtml, 6/18/11]

B)-"FACTORS" DEMONSTRATING RESIDENCY: Under the Oregon Act, the following constitute what the Act referred to as "factors" demonstrating residency:

> **Residency requirement.**
> Only requests made by Oregon residents … shall be granted. Factors demonstrating Oregon residency include but are not limited to:
> (1) Possession of an **Oregon driver license**;
> (2) **Registration to vote** in Oregon;
> (3) Evidence that the person **owns or leases property** in Oregon; *or*
> (4) Filing of an **Oregon tax return** for the most recent tax year.
>
> [ODWDA 127.860 §3.10 (emphasis supplied)]

C)-ADDITIONAL PROOFS: The above set forth "factors" are proceeded by the phrase "include but are not limited to." The meaning of this term is that the four enunciated factors are only examples, and satisfying all four of these factors is not required for a determination of Oregon residency, but each would be of primary importance.

As to the Oregon Department of Revenue's "permanent home" requirement, proofs would include: the ownership of a home or a lease on an apartment. That may include a gas/electric account, a land line telephone contract, TV and computer service, the purchase of furniture, and other forms of proof incident to the home/apartment's use.

The Oregon Division of Motor Vehicles, in addition to a driver's license, also requires the registration of automobiles.

As to the Oregon Department of Revenue's "center of your financial…life," a bank account and a brokerage account would apply.

D)-NO RESIDENCY PERIOD: The Oregon Act is silent as to any required residency period. Of course, the longer a patient has resided in the State of Oregon, the easier it is to prove residency.

E)-LONG TERM PHYSICIAN-PATIENT RELATIONSHIP: From a practical and evidentiary perspective, one of the best factors in establishing Oregon residency is a long term relationship between the physician and patient. Non-residents of Oregon may not avail themselves of the Oregon Death with Dignity Act.

F)-PHYSICIAN'S DOCUMENT RESPONSIBILITY: Because the Oregon Act requires residency, and because the attending physician is responsible for obtaining proof of residency from the patient, all forms of proof should be assembled prior to a first meeting with the physician.

§1.04)-"CAPABLE"

A QUALIFIED PATIENT MUST BE "CAPABLE" OF HAVING THE ABILITY TO MAKE AND COMMUNICATE HEALTH CARE DECISIONS.

Under the Oregon Act a patient must be "capable" of communicating his or her health care decisions.

> **"Capable"** means that in the opinion of a court or in the opinion of the patient's attending physician or consulting physician, psychiatrist or psychologist, a patient has the ability to make and communicate health care decisions to health care providers, including communication through persons familiar with the patient's manner of communicating if those persons are available.
>
> [ODWDA 127.800§1.01(3) (emphasis supplied)]

A)-ABILITY TO COMMUNICATE: In those cases where a patient cannot communicate directly with the physician because of speech impediments or other condition, such communications can be accomplished through a "person[] familiar with the patient's manner of communicating."

B)-ABILITY TO UNDERSTAND: In addition to the requirement that a patient must be able to communicate health care decisions, a further requirement is that the patient must be able to understand his/her medical "diagnosis and prognosis." This requirement originated within the context of a consulting physician's responsebility to provide a second opinion based on these factors. [ODWDA 127.800 §1.01(4)]

C)-VOLUNTARY DECISION: The Oregon Act is concerned with the risk of a patient making a decision as a result of undue influence. This concern is expressed in the Act's section on "Who may initiate a written request for medication," which states: "An adult … who has voluntarily expressed his or her wish to die." [ODWDA 127.805 §2.01(1)]

§1.05)-"INFORMED DECISION"

AN "INFORMED DECISION" IS MORE THAN "INFORMED CONSENT".

A patient must be capable of making an "informed decision." Under the Oregon Act an informed decision must be based on the following:

> **"Informed decision"** means a decision by a qualified patient, to request and obtain a prescription to end his or her life in a humane and dignified manner, that is based on an **appreciation of the relevant facts** and **after being fully informed by the attending physician** of: (a) His or her medical diagnosis; (b) His or her prognosis; (c) The potential risks associated with taking the medication to be prescribed; (d) The probable result of taking the medication to be prescribed; and (e) The feasible **alternatives**, including, but not limited to, comfort care, **hospice** care and pain control.
>
> [ODWDA 127.800§1.01(7) (emphasis supplied)]

A)-INFORMED CONSENT: For the purposes of a patient making an "informed consent" a physician must provide a general description of the nature of the procedure along with risks and alternatives. The physician must then ask the patient if he/she has any questions and then respond to these inquires.

B)-INFORMED DECISION: The burden on the physician in the case of an informed decision is greater that informed consent. In addition to providing a general description, the physician must also inform the patient of those details that would have been supplied upon request in the instance of an informed consent. In other words, the physician has no choice but to provide the details whether or not the patient initiates the request.

§1.06)-TERMINAL DISEASE

A TERMINAL DISEASE IS ONE THAT IS INCURABLE, IRREVERSIBLE AND WILL PRODUCE DEATH WITH-IN SIX MONTHS.

To be a qualified patient he/she must have a terminal disease:

> **Who may initiate a written request for medication.**
> An adult who is capable, is a resident of Oregon, and has been determined by the attending physician and consulting physician to be suffering from a **terminal disease**….
>
> [ODWDA 127.805§2.01(1) (emphasis supplied)]

At other places in the Oregon Act the term "illness" is used instead of the term "disease," without distinction.

A)-TERMINAL DISEASE-DEFINED: The Oregon Act defines terminal disease as a period of time:

> **"Terminal disease"** means an **incurable** and **irreversible** disease that has been medically confirmed and will, within reasonable medical judgment, produce **death within six months**.
>
> [ODWDA 127.800§1.01(12) (emphasis supplied)]

B)-PREDICTING SIX MONTH PERIOD: As set forth above, one element in the definition of a terminal disease is that it will "produce death within six months." This requirement is couched in terms of a "reasonable medical judgment." It can be noted that the six month element is also applicable for hospice care:

> In the United States, people with Medicare (and most other private insurance) can receive hospice care if their doctor believes that they most likely have less than 6 months to live if their illness runs a normal or typical course. … If the patient lives longer … the doctor and the hospice team will re-certify that the patient is terminally ill and that hospice services are appropriate. There is no

end to the hospice benefit under Medicare if the patient continues to meet the "expected within the next 6 months" criteria.

[http://www.eldercareteam.com/public/639.cfm]

§1.07)-SOUND JUDGMENT

TO BE A QUALIFIED PATIENT, ONE MUST NOT BE SUFFERING FROM A PSYCHIATRIC OR PSYCHO-LOGICAL DISORDER OR DEPRESSION CAUSING IMPAIRED JUDGMENT.

A principal safeguard in the Oregon Death with Dignity Act is the requirement that the patient have sound judgment, as phrased in the negative: "the patient is not suffering from a psychiatric or psychological disorder or depression causing impaired judgment." Note that the operative phrase is "impaired judgment." Thus, it is to be expected that patients facing the end of their lives from terminal diseases, with no more than six months to live, with many in extreme pain, will be depressed. But it is only depression which causes "impaired judgment" that disqualifies a patient.

> **Counseling referral.**
> If in the opinion of the attending physician or the consulting physician a patient may be <u>suffering from a psychiatric or psychological disorder or depression causing impaired judgment</u>, either physician shall refer the patient for counseling. No medication to end a patient's life in a humane and dignified manner shall be prescribed until the person performing the counseling determines that the patient is not suffering from a psychiatric or psychological disorder or depression causing impaired judgment.
> [ODWDA 127.825§3.03 emphasis supplied]

It should be noted that "impaired judgment," as used in the Oregon Act, is not equivalent to the concept of lack of testamentary capacity.

§1.08)-"COUNSELING"

COUNSELING MEANS BEING SEEN BY A STATE LICENSED PSYCHIATRIST OR PSYCHOLOGIST TO DETERMINE IF THE PATIENT IS CAPABLE.

The previous section, dealing with the requirement for a sound mind, discussed the need for a counseling referral in the event that a physician has concluded that a patient "may" be "suffering from a psychiatric or psychological disorder or depression causing impaired judgment." As to what constitutes counseling, the Oregon Act states:

> **"Counseling"** means <u>one or more consultations</u> as necessary between a <u>state licensed psychiatrist or psychologist</u> and a patient for the purpose of determining that the patient is capable and not suffering from a psychiatric or psychological disorder or depression causing impaired judgment.
>
> [ODWDA 127.800§1.01(5) (emphasis supplied)]

A)-STATE LICENSED PROFESSIONALS: Only psychiatrists and psychologists licensed in the State of Oregon are permitted to conduct the counseling evaluations under the Oregon Act.

B)-COUNSELING STATISTIC

In the first thirteen years (1998-2010) that the Oregon Act was in effect, of the 525 patients that were provided with life ending medications, 39—(7%) had first been referred to counseling. This seven percent only deals with this 525 population, and does not reflect how many may have been referred to counseling and found to have been not capable, and thus were not qualified patients and therefore could not participate in the program.

The Washington Act's experience over the two year period it was in effect (2009-2010) had seen only 5 of its patients—(4%) being referred for counseling.

§1.09)-NON-QUALIFYING SOLELY AGE OR DISABILITY

NO PERSON SHALL QUALIFY ... SOLELY BE-CAUSE OF AGE OR DISABILITY

As stated earlier in the chapter, one of the requirements to be a qualified patient is having a terminal disease.

To emphasize this point, the Oregon Act states that no one can become a qualified patient solely because of age or disability.

> No person shall qualify ... solely because of age or disability.
>
> [ODWDA 127.805§2.01(2)]

[page left blank]

CHAPTER-TWO
PROCEDURES

OREGON DEATH WITH DIGNITY ACT ("ODWDA") or ("OREGON ACT")

TABLE OF CONTENTS

NOTE: This chapter/book does not contain legal or medical advice, which can only be obtained from the reader's personal attorney or physician.

§2.01)-QUALIFIED PATIENT

AS SET FORTH IN CHAPTER-ONE OF THIS BOOK, A "QUALIFIED PATIENT" IS: 1)-AN ADULT; 2)-CAPABLE; 3)-OREGON RESIDENT; 4)-SUFFERING FROM A TERMINAL DISEASE; 5)-WITH LESS THAN SIX MONTHS TO LIVE.

The Oregon Death with Dignity Act is only available to a "qualified patient." Chapter-One of this book details the required characteristics in order to achieve the classification of a qualified patient.

§2.02)-THREE REQUESTS

IN ORDER TO RECEIVE A PRESCRIPTION FOR MEDICATION TO END LIFE, A PATIENT MUST MAKE THREE REQUESTS: TWO ORALLY AND ONE IN WRITING.

The necessity of making three requests according to the Oregon Death with Dignity Act is stated as follows:

> **Written and oral requests.**
> In order to receive a prescription for medication to end his or her life in a humane and dignified manner, a qualified patient shall have made an <u>oral request</u> and a <u>written request</u>, and reiterate the oral request to his or her attending physician no less than fifteen (15) days after making the initial oral request. At the time the qualified patient makes his or her <u>second oral request</u>, the attending physician shall offer the patient an opportunity to rescind the request.
>
> [ODWDA 127.840§3.06 (emphasis supplied)]

A)-INITIAL ORAL REQUEST: To start the process under the Oregon Act, a qualified patient must make an initial oral request for a prescription for medication to end his or her life in a humane and dignified manner.

B)-WRITTEN REQUEST: After making the initial oral request, the qualified patient must make a written request in the form prescribed under the Act, and set forth later in this chapter.

C)-SECOND ORAL REQUEST: The qualified patient must make a second oral request.

D)-WAITING PERIODS: The Oregon Act provides two waiting periods:

> **Waiting periods.**
> No less than fifteen (15) days shall elapse between the patient's initial oral request and the writing of a prescription under [the ODWDA]. No less than 48 hours shall elapse between the patient's written request and the writing of a prescription under [the ODWDA].
> [ODWDA 127.850§3.08 (emphasis supplied)]

E)-15 DAY PROCESS: The fastest that the system can work is 15 days using the following timing:

> first)-make the initial oral request on day-one;
> second)-make the written request within the next thirteen days; and
> third)-make the second oral request fifteen days after the first oral request.

§2.03)-RIGHT TO RESCIND

A PATIENT MAY ALWAYS RESCIND HIS/HER REQUEST FOR MEDICATION AND THE PHYSICIAN MUST PROVIDE THE OPPORTUNITY.

One of the safeguards in the Oregon Act is the requirement that the physician give the patient the right to rescind upon receiving the second oral request, and that the patient always has the right to rescind thereafter. If any time elapses between the second oral request and the writing of the prescription, the physician must offer the qualified patient another opportunity to rescind.

> **Right to rescind request.**
> A patient may rescind his or her request at any time and in any manner without regard to his or her mental state. No prescription for medication under [the ODWDA] may be written without the attending physician offering the qualified patient an opportunity to rescind the request.
>
> [ODWDA 127.845§3.07 (emphasis supplied)]

§2.04)-CONSULTING PHYSICIAN

TWO PHYSICIANS MUST VERIFY THE TERMINAL DISEASE OF THE QUALIFIED PATIENT: FIRST THE ATTENDING PHYSICIAN AND THEN A CONSULTING PHYSICIAN.

A safeguard of the Oregon Act is the requirement that the opinion of the attending physician be backed up by a second physician—called the consulting physician

> **Consulting physician confirmation.**
> Before a patient is qualified under [the ODWDA], a consulting physician shall examine the patient and his or her relevant medical records and confirm, in writing, the attending physician's diagnosis that the patient is suffering from a terminal disease, and verify that the patient is capable, is acting voluntarily and has made an informed decision.
>
> [ODWDA 127.820§3.02]

§2.05)-FORM OF WRITTEN REQUEST

A WRITTEN REQUEST MUST BE IN THE FORM PROVIDED IN THE ACT, AND CONTAIN TWO WITNESSES.

The Oregon Act contains a form that must be followed in order for a qualified patient to make a written request:

REQUEST FOR MEDICATION TO END MY LIFE IN A HUMANE AND DIGNIFIED MANNER

I, _____, am an adult of sound mind.

I am suffering from _____, which my attending physician has determined is a terminal disease and which has been medically confirmed by a consulting physician.

I have been fully informed of my diagnosis, prognosis, the nature of medication to be prescribed and potential associated risks, the expected result, and the feasible alternatives, including comfort care, hospice care and pain control.

I request that my attending physician prescribe medication that will end my life in a humane and dignified manner.

INITIAL ONE:

_____ I have informed my family of my decision and taken their opinions into consideration.

_____ I have decided not to inform my family of my decision.

_____ I have no family to inform of my decision.

I understand that I have the right to rescind this request at any time.

I understand the full import of this request and I expect to die when I take the medication to be prescribed. I further understand that although most deaths occur within three hours, my death may take longer and my physician has counseled me about this possibility.

I make this request voluntarily and without reservation, and I accept full moral responsibility for my actions.

Signed: _____
Dated: _____

[ODWDA 127.897§6.01]

A)-AFTER CONSULTING PHYSICIAN: Note that the written request cannot be prepared until after a consulting physician has confirmed the presence of the terminal disease. Thus, to keep the waiting periods as short as possible it is important to obtain the opinion of the consulting physician as soon as possible.

B)-TWO WITNESSES—ONE INDEPENDENT: The written request must be witnessed by two witnesses, and at least one must be independent:

Form of the written request.

(1) A valid request for medication under [the ODWDA] shall be in substantially the form described in ORS 127.897, signed and dated by the patient and witnessed by at least two individuals who, in the presence of the patient, attest that to the best of their knowledge and belief the patient is capable, acting voluntarily, and is not being coerced to sign the request.

(2) One of the witnesses shall be a person who is not: (a) A relative of the patient by blood, marriage or adoption; (b) A person who at the time the request is signed would be entitled to any portion of the estate of the qualified patient upon death under any will or by operation of law; or (c) An owner, operator or employee of a health care facility where the qualified patient is receiving medical treatment or is a resident.

(3) The patient's attending physician at the time the request is signed shall not be a witness.

[ODWDA 127.810§2.02 (emphasis supplied)]

C)-LONG TERM CARE FACILITY: If the patient is in a long term care facility one of the two witnesses must be from that facility:

> If the patient is a patient in a long term care facility at the time the written request is made, one of the witnesses shall be an individual designated by the facility and having the qualifications specified by the Department of Human Services by rule.
>
> [ODWDA 127.810§2.02(4)]

§2.06)-THE ODWDA IS NOT ASSISTED-SUICIDE

THE OREGON DEATH WITH DIGNITY ACT DOES NOT CONSTITUTE SUICIDE, ASSISTED SUICIDE, MERCY KILLING OR HOMICIDE.

The Oregon Death with Dignity Act is crystal clear that the patient's actions, and those of the physicians, do not constitute suicide, assisted suicide, mercy killing or homicide:

> **Construction of Act.**
> Actions taken in accordance with [the ODWDA] shall not, for any purpose, constitute suicide, assisted suicide, mercy killing or homicide, under the law.
>
> [ODWDA 127.880§3.14]

§2.07)-EUTHANASIA IS HOMICIDE

ACTIONS TAKEN BY A PHYSICIAN OUTSIDE THE SPECIFIC PROVISIONS OF THE OREGON DEATH WITH DIGNITY ACT CAN CONSTITUTE HOMI-CIDE.

As stated above, a physician's actions under the ODWDA do not constitute assisted suicide, mercy killing or homicide. But, actions by a physician outside the Act can constitute homicide. An example of actions that can constitute homicide can be found in the following subsection on euthanasia.

A)-HOMICIDE: Under Oregon law, as well as the law in all fifty states, euthanasia is homicide.

> **Construction of Act.**
> Nothing in [the ODWDA] shall be construed to authorize a physician or any other person to end a patient's life by <u>lethal injection</u>, mercy killing or active euthanasia.
> [ODWDA 127.880§3.14 (emphasis supplied)]

B)-EUTHANASIA: The all important distinction between "physician-assisted death"—specifically made legal under the Oregon Death with Dignity Act, and "euthanasia"—specifically excluded from the Act and thus presumably prosecutable as homicide, revolves around the issue of who administers the medication. When the patient self-administers the medication— physician-assisted death; when the physician or other individual administers the medication—homicide.

C)-ADMINISTERS MEDICATION: It is easy to differentiate between, on the one hand, a patient on his/her own drinking the medication, and on the other hand a physician providing a lethal injection. What is not so easy to discern is when allowable assistance become unlawful administration. That is the subject of the next section.

§2.08)-SELF ADMINISTRATION AND ASSISTANCE

UNDER THE OREGON DEATH WITH DIGNITY ACT A PATIENT MUST SELF-ADMINISTER THE MEDICATION TO END HIS/HER LIFE.

A patient, and only the patient, must self-administer the medication to end his/her life. As stated in the written request for the medication:

> **Request for medication.**
> "I understand the full import of this request and I expect to die when I take the medication to be prescribed."
> [ODWDA 127.897§6.01]

A)-ASSISTANCE: The Oregon Death with Dignity Act does not provide guidance as to what actions on the part of another person (physician, healthcare provider, or other individual) will be construed as allowable assistance and what will constitute unlawful administration.

The history of Dr. Jack Kevorkian is instructive. On numerous occasions Dr. Kevorkian was put on trial for physician-assisted suicide, only to be acquitted each time. In all these instances, he mixed a lethal dose of medication in a machine, attached the machine to the patient, and then let the patient push the final button that delivered the medication and brought about death. Thus, in the final instance, the patient always self-administered the lethal dose of medication.

Then, Dr. Kevorkian decided to push the envelope, by being the individual that actually pushed the button without assistance from the patient. He was then prosecuted and convicted of homicide.

The lesson, as it pertains to the Oregon Death with Dignity Act, is that individuals can assist in providing some form of very limited physical assistance, but the patient must remain in complete control of the decision, timing and actually taking the lethal dose of medication. Control over the decision and the timing are easy to determine. The action of taking the medication is more difficult to measure. As long as the patient has the capacity to swallow, it might be allowable for an individual to hold the glass up to the patient's mouth or other types of very limited physical assistance.

B)-DEATH AT HOME WITHOUT A PHYSICIAN: As will be more fully seen in Chapter-Three Statistics, out of 525 patients 498—(95%) chose to die at home, and in those instances the prescribing physician was present 21 percent of the time. As a practical matter, it might be easier for a member of the patient's immediate family to provide required assistance.

§2.09)-FAMILY NOTIFICATION

IT IS RECOMMENDED THAT A PATIENT NOTIFY NEXT OF KIN, BUT FAILURE TO DO SO MAY NOT BE HELD AGAINST THE PATIENT.

The Oregon Act recommends that a patient notify his/her family of the decision, but the patient cannot be penalized for declining the recommendation.

> **Family notification.**
> The attending physician shall recommend that the patient notify the next of kin of his or her request for medication pursuant to [the ODWDA]. A patient who declines or is unable to notify next of kin shall not have his or her request denied for that reason.
>
> [ODWDA 127.835§3.05]

§2.10)-WILLS, CONTRACTS AND STATUTES

NO PROVISION IN ANY WILL, CONTRACT OR OTHER AGREEMENT SHALL AFFECT THE USE OF THE OREGON DEATH WITH DIGNITY ACT.

The Oregon Act is sacrosanct in that it cannot be affected by contrary provisions in wills, contracts and other agreements. Thus, for example, if a contract states that it will be invalid if a contracting party utilizes the Oregon Death with Dignity Act, said provision would be null and void.

> **Effect on construction of wills, contracts and statutes.**
> (1) No provision in a contract, will or other agreement, whether written or oral, to the extent the provision would affect whether a person may make or rescind a request for medication to end his or her life in a humane and dignified manner, shall be valid.
> (2) No obligation owing under any currently existing contract shall be conditioned or affected by the making or rescinding of a request, by a person, for medication to end his or her life in a humane and dignified manner.
>
> [ODWDA 127.870§3.12]

§2.11)-INSURANCE AND ANNUITY POLICIES

THE USE OF THE OREGON DEATH WITH DIGNITY DOES NOT HAVE ANY EFFECT ON INSURANCE POLICIES.

The employment of the Oregon Act to bring about the death of an insured cannot be used by an insurance company to negate the insurance policy's coverage. For example, it would seem to be the case that an insurance policy with a provision negating coverage if the insured commits suicide within the first one or two years could not be used if the insured terminates his/her own life pursuant to the Oregon Act. Similarly, it would appear that a life insurance policy could not be abrogated by the insured's use of the Oregon Act.

> **Insurance or annuity policies.**
> The sale, procurement, or issuance of any life, health, or accident insurance or annuity policy or the rate charged for any policy shall not be conditioned upon or affected by the making or rescinding of a request, by a person, for medication to end his or her life in a humane and dignified manner. Neither shall a qualified patient's act of ingesting medication to end his or her life in a humane and dignified manner have an effect upon a life, health, or accident insurance or annuity policy.
>
> [ODWDA 127.875§3.13 (emphasis supplied)]

§2.12)-IMMUNITIES AND LIABILITIES

A PHYSICIAN OR OTHER INDIVIDUAL TAKING ACTIONS IN ACCORDANCE WITH THE OREGON ACT IS IMMUNE FROM CIVIL OR CRIMINAL LIABILITY.

While the Oregon Act specifies that it does not constitute "suicide, assisted suicide, mercy killing or homicide," the Act goes on to specify that actions taken under the Act cannot be the basis for civil or criminal liability. Thus, physicians and other individuals can dismiss any lawsuit brought by an aggrieved relative of the patient for negligence, and can prevail over a prosecution for homicide or other battery. These immunities can be claimed for those "participating in good faith compliance".

---

permissible sanctions.
Except as provided in [the ODWDA]:
　　(1) <u>No person shall be subject to civil or criminal liability</u> or professional disciplinary action for participating in good faith compliance with [the ODWDA]. This includes being present when a qualified patient takes the prescribed medication to end his or her life in a humane and dignified manner.
　　. . . . .
　　(3) <u>No request</u> by a patient for or provision by an attending physician of medication in good faith compliance with the provisions of [the ODWDA] <u>shall constitute neglect</u> for any purpose of law or provide the sole basis for the appointment of a guardian or conservator.

[ODWDA 127.885§4.01 (emphasis supplied)]

---

§2.13)-CONSCIENTIOUS OBJECTION

<u>NO ONE IS FORCED TO PARTICIPATE IN THE OREGON DEATH WITH DIGNITY ACT. THOSE WITH A CONSCIENTIOUS OBJECTION MAY ABSTAIN WITHOUT PENALTY.</u>

There are those who oppose the Oregon Death with Dignity Act on moral grounds and under no circumstances would agree to participate in providing qualified patients with lethal doses of medication to end their lives. These individuals can be physicians, psychiatrists, psychologists, and any other health care provider.

These individuals are conscientious objectors, and have the absolute right to abstain from participation.

> **Immunities; basis for prohibiting health care provider from participation; notification; permissible sanctions.**
> (2) No professional organization or association, or health care provider, may subject a person to censure, discipline, suspension, loss of license, loss of privileges, loss of membership or other penalty for participating or refusing to participate in good faith compliance with [the ODWDA].
> [ODWDA 127.885§4.01 (emphasis supplied)1]

§2.14)-DEATH IN A PUBLIC PLACE
THE OREGON DEATH WITH DIGNITY ACT IMPOSES PENALTIES FOR PATIENTS WHO CHOOSE TO DIE IN A PUBLIC PLACE.

The Oregon Act provides penalties against those patients who terminate their lives in a public place:

> **Claims by governmental entity for costs incurred.**
> Any governmental entity that incurs costs resulting from a person terminating his or her life pursuant to the provisions of [the ODWDA] in a public place shall have a claim against the estate of the person to recover such costs and reasonable attorney fees related to enforcing the claim.
> [ODWDA 127.892 (emphasis supplied)1]

§2.15)-CRIMINAL PENALTIES
IT IS A CLASS-A FELONY TO WILLFULLY ALTER, FORGE, CONCEAL OR DESTROY A DOCUMENT CREATED PURSUANT TO THE OREGON DEATH WITH DIGNITY ACT.

A Class A Felony in the State of Oregon is punishable by a prison sentence of up to twenty years. [Oregon Criminal Law, §161.605] The "penalties" section in the Oregon Death with Dignity Act specified the following:

> **Penalties.**
>
> (1) It shall be a **Class A felony** for a person without authorization of the principal to <u>willfully alter, forge, conceal or destroy an instrument</u>, the reinstatement or revocation of an instrument or any other evidence or document reflecting the principal's desires and interests, <u>with the intent and effect of causing a withholding or withdrawal of life sustaining procedures or of artificially administered nutrition and hydration which</u> **hastens the death** of the principal.
>
> (2) Except as provided in subsection (1) of this section, it shall be a **Class A misdemeanor** for a person without authorization of the principal to <u>willfully alter, forge, conceal or destroy an instrument</u>, the reinstatement or revocation of an instrument, or any other evidence or document <u>reflecting the principal's desires and interests</u> <u>with the intent or effect of affecting a health care decision</u>.
>
> [ODWDA 127.995 (emphasis supplied)1]

§2.16)-INITIATING THE CONVERSATION

<u>AS BETWEEN THE PATIENT AND THE PHYSICIAN, IT IS THE PATIENT'S RESPONSIBILITY TO INITIATE THE CONVERSATION REGARDING THE OREGON DEATH WITH DIGNITY ACT.</u>

A patient has many end-of-life options, one of which is the Oregon Death with Dignity Act. Awareness of this option is the problem. As between the patient and the physician it might be the patient's responsibility to initiate the discussion.

A physician might initiate the conversation with his/her patient regarding the Oregon Death with Dignity Act. But then again, the physician might refrain from initiating this discussion because of the appearance of undue influence.

§2.17)-ATTENDING PHYSICIAN RESPONSIBILITIES

THE ATTENDING PHYSICIAN HAS THE RESPONSIBILITY OF INSURING COMPLIANCE WITH ALL THE PROVISIONS OF THE OREGON DEATH WITH DIGNITY ACT

A separate section of the Oregon Act is entitled "Attending physician responsibilities." In essence, the attending physician is the Act's administrator.

Set forth below is the section regarding the attending physician's responsibilities, with captions added as shown in brackets "[]."

Attending physician responsibilities.
(1) The attending physician shall:
[INITIAL DETERMINATION] (a) Make the initial determination of whether a patient has a terminal disease, is capable, and has made the request voluntarily;
[OREGON RESIDENCY] (b) Request that the patient demonstrate Oregon residency;
[INFORMED DECISION] (c) To ensure that the patient is making an informed decision, inform the patient of: (A) His or her medical diagnosis; (B) His or her prognosis; (C) The potential risks associated with taking the medication to be prescribed; (D) The probable result of taking the medication to be prescribed; and (E) The feasible alternatives, including, but not limited to, comfort care, hospice care and pain control;
[CONSULTING PHYSICIAN] (d) Refer the patient to a consulting physician for medical confirmation of the

---

diagnosis, and for a determination that the patient is capable and acting voluntarily;

[COUNSELING] (e) Refer the patient for counseling if appropriate ...;

[NOTIFY FAMILY] (f) Recommend that the patient notify next of kin;

[PRESENCE OF ANOTHER PERSON] (g) Counsel the patient about the importance of having another person present when the patient takes the medication prescribed ....

[PUBLIC PLACE] and of not taking the medication in a public place;

[OFFER TO RESCIND] (h) Inform the patient that he or she has an opportunity to rescind the request at any time and in any manner, and offer the patient an opportunity to rescind at the end of the 15 day waiting period ...;

[INFORMED DECISION] (i) Verify, immediately prior to writing the prescription for medication ..., that the patient is making an informed decision;

[MEDICAL RECORDS] (j) Fulfill the medical record documentation requirements ...; (k) Ensure that all appropriate steps are carried out ... prior to writing a prescription for medication to enable a qualified patient to end his or her life in a humane and dignified manner; and

[DISPENSING MEDICATIONS] (l) (A) Dispense medications directly, including ancillary medications intended to facilitate the desired effect to minimize the patient's discomfort, provided the attending physician is registered as a dispensing physician with the Oregon Medical Board, has a current Drug Enforcement Administration certificate and complies with any applicable administrative rule; or

[PHARMACIST] (B) With the patient's written consent: (i) Contact a pharmacist and inform the pharmacist of the prescription; and (ii) Deliver the written prescription personally or by mail to the pharmacist, who will dispense the medications to either the patient, the attending physician or an expressly identified agent of the patient.

[DEATH CERTIFICATE] (2) Notwithstanding any other provision of law, the attending physician may sign the patient's death certificate.

[ODWDA 127.815§3.01 (captions supplied)]

§2.18)-STATISTICES—CHAPTER THREE

The next chapter in this book discusses the statistical history of the Oregon Death with Dignity Act.

CHAPTER-THREE
STATISTICS
1998-2010 13 YEARS 525 PATIENTS
OREGON DEATH WITH DIGNITY ACT
("ODWDA") or ("Oregon Act")

TABLE OF CONTENTS

NOTE: This chapter/book does not contain legal or medical advice, which can only be obtained from the reader's personal attorney or physician.

INTRODUCTION

OREGON STATISTICS—("ODWDA"): As of January 7, 2011, the State of Oregon had thirteen years of experience with the Oregon Death with Dignity Act ("ODWDA") or simply the "Oregon Act." The Oregon Public Health Division published a report entitled: "Characteristics and end-of-life care of 525 DWDA patients who died after ingesting a lethal dose of medication as of January 7, 2011." The statistics derived from this report are summarized in the below text, and the detailed tables that follow.

STAND ALONE CHAPTER: This chapter is meant to stand alone, meaning that some material in the commentary is repeated at other places of this book.

WASHINGTON STATISTICS—("WDWDA"): Frequent references will be made to statistics from the Washington Death with Dignity Act ("WDWDA") or simply the "Washington Act." This Act went into effect in March of 2009, and for the years of 2009-2010 there were 119 patients.

§3.01)-RESIDENCE REQUIREMENT
A)-TABLE-1
RESIDENCE

	1998-2010 (N-525)	1998-2010 %
Metro counties	226	43.05
Coastal counties	41	7.81
Other western counties	219	41.71
East of the Cascades	39	7.43
totals	*525*	*100.00*

As can be seen, all 525 ODWDA patients resided in the State of Oregon. The Oregon Act contains a residency requirement:

> **Who may initiate a written request for medication.** An adult who [is] a resident of Oregon....
> [ODWDA 127.805 §2.01(1)]

B)-PROOF OF RESIDENCE: The Act contains "factors demonstrating Oregon residency." The qualifying language states "included but … not limited to," meaning that other proofs will be considered. These enumerated factors are:

> (1) Possession of an <u>Oregon driver license</u>;
> (2) <u>Registration to vote</u> in Oregon;
> (3) Evidence that the person <u>owns or leases property</u> in Oregon; or
> (4) Filing of an <u>Oregon tax return</u> for the most recent tax year.
>
> [ODWDA 127.860 §3.10]

C)-DURATION OF PATIENT-PHYSICIAN RELATIONSHIP

As will be discussed at length in §3.06, entitled "Timing of Event," the median (mid-point) of the patient-physician relationship was just 10 weeks, with a range of 0-1905 weeks. Thus, if other evidence of residency can be established, a lengthy patient-physician relationship may not be required.

§3.02)-UNDERLYING ILLNESS
A)-TABLE-2

UNDERLYING ILLNESS

	1998-2010 (N-525)	1998-2010 %
Malignant neoplasms [cancer]	424	80.76
Lung and bronchus	96	18.29
Pancreas	38	7.24
Breast	41	7.81
Colon	34	6.48
Prostate	25	4.76
Other	190	36.19
Amyotrophic lateral sclerosis-ALS	42	8.00
Chronic lower respiratory disease	20	3.81
HIV/AIDS	8	1.52
Other illnesses	31	5.90
totals	*525*	*100.00*

B)-CANCER—81%: By far and away the most numerous underlying illnesses in the 525 ODWDA population is cancer—424 patients—(81%). This cancer category is subdivided into six subcategories: lung and bronchus-96 patients—(18%), pancreas-38 patients—(7%), breast-41 patients—(8%), colon-34 patients—(6%), prostate-25 patients—(5%), and other-190 patients—(36%).

The cancer deaths experienced under the Washington Act mirror the above statistic for cancer-(78%).

C)-ALS—8%: The next largest group is those with amyotrophic lateral sclerosis (ALS), also known as Lou Gehrig's disease-42 patients—(8%). The deaths experienced under the Washington Act for what is there referred to as "Neuro-degenerative disease (incl. ALS)," is a like—(9%).

D)-HIV/AIDS—2%: Those with HIV/AIDS-8 patients—(2%) were third in number.

§3.03)-END OF LIFE CONCERNS
A)-TABLE-3
END OF LIFE CONCERNS

	1998-2010 (N-525)	1998-2010 %
Losing Autonomy	475	90.48
Less able to engage in activities making life enjoyable	459	87.43
Loss of dignity	333	63.43
Losing control of bodily functions	294	56.00
Burden on family, friends/caregivers	184	35.05
Inadequate pain control or concern	111	21.14
Financial implications of treatment	13	2.48
totals	N/A	N/A

Of the 525 ODWDA population, 475 patients—(90%) named "losing autonomy" as their principal end of life concern; 459

patients—(87%) mentioned being "less able to engage in activities making life enjoyable;" more than half-333 patients—(63%) cited "loss of dignity;" and 294 patients—(56%) worried about "losing control of bodily functions."

On the issue of how their condition affected others, 184 patients—(35%) mentioned being a "burden on family friends/ caregivers."

"Inadequate pain control or concern about it" affected 111 patients—(21%).

Only 13 patients—(2%) worried about "financial implications of treatment." This should be cross-referenced to the fact that 2 percent of the 525 population had no insurance whatsoever.

B)-WASHINGTON STATISTICS: Patients under the Washington Act expressed like concerns as can be seen from the following comparison.

END OF LIFE CONCERNS: OREGON & WASHINGTON

	OREGON ACT (N-525) %	WASHINGTON ACT (N-119) %
Losing Autonomy	90.48	87.39
Less able to engage in activities making life enjoyable	87.43	82.35
Loss of dignity	63.43	66.39
Losing control of bodily functions	56.00	44.54
Burden on family, friends/caregivers	35.05	24.37
Inadequate pain control or concern	21.14	29.41
Financial implications of treatment	2.48	3.36
totals	*N/A*	*N/A*

§3.04)-END OF LIFE CARE
A)-TABLE-4

END OF LIFE CARE

	1998-2010	1998-2010
	(N-525)	%
Hospice		
Enrolled	454	86.48
Not enrolled	58	11.05
*Unknow*n	13	2.48
totals	*525*	*100.00*
Insurance		
Private	351	66.86
Medicare/Medicaid/Governm't	157	29.90
None	8	1.52
*Unknow*n	9	1.71
totals	*525*	*100.00*

B)-HOSPICE CARE—86%: Of the 525 ODWDA population, a full 454 patients—(86%) were enrolled in hospice at the time they made the decision to end their lives by ingesting a lethal dose of medication. This statistic is surprising to those who hold to the belief that hospice is an effective alternative to the death with dignity acts. Even more surprising is the fact that in 2007, the average (median) stay in an Oregon hospice program was only 18 days between admission and death. [*A Guidebook for Health Care Professionals*, sec. 4, cited in Appendix A.17 of this book]

1)-SUPREME COURT: In the 1997 Supreme Court case of Washington v. Glucksberg, the Coalition of Hospice Professionals filed an *Amici Curiae*—friend of the court—brief citing studies showing that: "[a]s death becomes more imminent, pain and suffering become progressively more difficult to treat") [Glucksberg at 748] To this observation regarding hospice care at the end of life, Justice Stevens in his concurring opinion stated: "An individual adequately informed of the care alternatives thus might make a rational choice for assisted suicide." [Id]

2)-WASHINGTON ACT—79%: The Washington experience was similar with 79% enrolled in hospice.

C)-INSURANCE: The statistics concerning insurance hold several surprises. Although the median age of the 525 ODWDA population was 71 (see §3.11), meaning that half of the 525 (262) should have been on Medicare, only 157 patients (30%) had Medicare/Medicaid or other government insurance. Perhaps there was some confusion with the fact that 351 patients (67%) had private insurance, which insurance might have been in addition to Medicare. It was also a surprise that only 8 patients (2%) had no insurance.

§3.05)-PROCESS
A)-TABLE-5
PROCESS

	1998-2010	1998-2010
	(N-525)	%
Patient died at:		
Home (patient, family or friend)	498	94.86
Long term care	21	4.00
Hospital	1	.19
Other	5	.95
totals	525	100.00
Lethal medication		
Secobarbital	321	61.14
Pentobarbital	200	38.10
Other	4	.76
totals	525	100.00
Referred for psychiatric evaluation	39	7.43
Patient informed family of decision	423	80.57

B)-PLACE OF DEATH: Of the 525 ODWDA population practically all, 498 patients—(95%), elected to die at either their own homes or those of a family member or close friend. Because the ingestion of the lethal dose of medication acted so quickly, there was less of a burden in choosing this most personal place to die. The Washington Act saw 92% chose a like environment to die.

C)-LETHAL MEDICATION: The two lethal medications prescribed were Secobarbital for 321 patients—(61%), and Pentobarbital for 200 patients—(38%), and a combination of the two and/or morphine for the remaining 4 patients—(<1%). Washington patients also chose Secobarbital—92% and Pentabarbital—7%.

D)-PSYCHIATRIC EVALUATION: Thirty nine patients—(7%) were referred for psychiatric evaluation in accordance with the Act's requirement for a "counseling referral":

> **Counseling referral.**
> If in the opinion of the attending physician or the consulting physician a patient may be suffering from a psychiatric or psychological disorder or depression causing impaired judgment, either physician shall refer the patient for counseling. No medication to end a patient's life in a humane and dignified manner shall be prescribed until the person performing the counseling determines that the patient is not suffering from a psychiatric or psychological disorder or **depression causing impaired judgment**.
>
> [ODWDA 127.825 §3.03 (emphasis supplied)]

Psychiatric evaluations under the Washington Act amounted to only 4%, almost half of the Oregon referrals.

E)-DEPRESSION: Of course, depression can be expected to be present as patients face the reality of a terminal illness with less than six months to live, and experience the "end of life concerns" set forth in §3.03 above, However, it should be noted that it is not just "depression" that is at issue, but a "depression causing impaired judgment," a much higher standard.

F)-FAMILY NOTIFICATION: Most of the patients-423—(81%) elected to inform their families of their decision. The Act only requires the attending physician to "recommend" such disclosure; the patient is under no obligation to make that notification:

> **Family notification.** The attending physician shall recommend that the patient notify the next of kin of his or her request for medication pursuant to .... A patient who declines or is unable to notify next of kin shall not have his or her request denied for that reason.
>
> [ODWDA 127.835 §3.05]

The Washington patients chose to notify their families 85% of the time, similar to Oregon's 81%.

§3.06)-TIMING OF EVENT
A)-TABLE-6

TIMING OF EVENT

	1998-2010
	(N-525)
Duration (weeks) of patient-physician relationship	
Median	10
Range	0-1905
Unknown (20)	
Duration (days) between 1st request and death	
Median	46
Range	15-1009
Minutes between ingestion and unconsciousness	
Median	5
Range	1-38
Unknown (71)	
Minutes between ingestion and death	
Median	25
Range (minutes – hours)	1min-104hrs
Unknown (66)	

B)-PATIENT-PHYSICIAN RELATIONSHIP: The median (mid-point) duration of the patient-physician relationship was only 10 weeks (two and a half months), but the shortest time was measured in less than one week. The conclusion that can be drawn from these statistics is that in many cases the physician involved in the prescription of the lethal dose of medication had no long-term relationship with the patient.

C)-TIME BETWEEN 1ST REQUEST AND DEATH: The time between the first request for the prescription of the lethal dose of medication and death was a median of just 46 days—a month and a half. What this appears to indicate is that patients waited until almost the very end to make their choices to use the death with dignity acts.

D)-PHYSICIAN-ASSISTED DEATH—NOT SUICIDE: The word "suicide" does not appear anywhere in the Oregon Death with Dignity Act except in the following provision:

> **Construction of Act.**
> Nothing in [the Act] shall be construed to authorize a physician or any other person to end a patient's life by lethal injection, mercy killing or active euthanasia. <u>Actions taken in accordance with [the Act] shall not, for any purpose, constitute suicide, assisted suicide, mercy killing or homicide,</u> under the law.
>
> [ODWDA 127.880 §3.14 (emphasis supplied)]

Early press releases from the Oregon Public Health Division referred to the program as "physician assisted suicide." [e.g., OHD Press Releases 2/17/99, 2/21/01, 3/5/03] In the March 15, 2011, OHD press release the practice was referred to as "physician-assisted death."

E)-BETWEEN INGESTION AND DEATH: While the median (min-point) minutes between ingestion and unconsciousness are only 5, the remaining minutes until death are an additional 20. Thus, the median minutes between ingestion and death are 25. But the range is between one minute and 104 hours. In other words, a patient can linger as long as four days. The most frequent cause for these longer times is the problem of regurgitation.

§3.07)-HEALTH-CARE PROVIDER PRESENT
A)-TABLE-7
HEALTH-CARE PROVIDER PRESENT

	1998-2010	1998-2010
	(N-525)	%
When medication was ingested		
Prescribing physician	94	20.66
Other provider (prescribing physician not present)	228	50.11
No provider	67	14.73
Unknown	66	14.51
totals	455	100.00
At time of death		
Prescribing physician	83	18.24
Other provider (prescribing physician not present)	252	55.38
No provider	108	23.74
Unknown	12	2.64
totals	455	100.00

B)-PHYSICIAN PRESENT—21%: In only 94 cases—(21%) was the prescribing physician present when the lethal medication was ingested. And then in only 83 cases—(18%) was the prescribing physician present at time of death. In the Washington experience, the prescribing physician was present when the lethal medication was ingested in only 6% of the cases.

C)-OTHER PROVIDER PRESENT—50%: In 228 cases—(50%) a provider other than the prescribing physician was present when the lethal medication was ingested. And then in 252 cases—(55%) was such provider present at the time of death. Thus in 335 cases—(74%) of the cases either the physician or a provider was present at the time of death. In the Washington experience, a provider other than the prescribing physician was present in 50% of the cases.

D)-NO PROVIDER PRESENT—15%: In 67 cases—(15%) no provider was present when the lethal medication was ingested. And then in 108 cases—(24%) no provider was present at the time of death. Of course this is not saying anything about which other individuals were present such as family members or friends.

E)-LETHAL MEDICATION SAFEGUARDS: What is not explained in the above statistics from the Oregon Public Health Division concerns the safeguards placed on the possession of lethal medication in those cases where no physician or provider is present at the time of ingestion. Absent from the Oregon Act, is a provision in the Washington Act entitled: "Disposal of unused medications," which goes on to specify: "Any medication dispensed under this chapter that was not self-administered shall be disposed of by lawful means." [WDWDA RCW 70.245.140]

§3.08)-COMPLICATIONS
A)-TABLE-8

COMPLICATIONS

	1998-2010	1998-2010
	(N-525)	%
No complication	456	86.86
Regurgitated	21	4.00
Seizures	0	0.00
Awakened after taking prescription	3	.57
Unknown	48	9.14
totals	*N/A*	*N/A*

B)-NO COMPLICATIONS—87%: No complications were experienced by 456 patients—(87%). The Washington figure is an almost identical 86%.

C)-REGURGITATION—4%: Regurgitation of the prescription was experienced by 21 patients—(4%). Not explained by the Oregon Public Health Division's report is what happened to these 21 patients. The Washington figure is only 1%.

D)-AWAKENING<1%: Awakened after taking the prescription were 3 patients (0.57%). The explanation set forth by the Oregon Public Health Division for this statistic was as follows: "In 2005, one patient regained consciousness 65 hours after ingesting the medication, subsequently dying from their illness 14 days after awakening. In 2010, two patients regained consciousness after ingesting medications. One patient regained consciousness 88 hours after ingesting the medication, subsequently dying from their illness three months later. The other patient regained consciousness within 24 hours, subsequently dying from their illness five days following ingestion."

§3.09)-EMERGENCY MEDICAL SERVICES
A)-TABLE-9
EMERGENCY MEDICAL SERVICES

	1998-2010	1998-2010
	(N-525)	%
Not called after medication ingested	479	91.24
Called for intervention	0	0.00
Calls for other reasons	4	.76
Unknown	42	8.00
totals	*525*	*100.00*

B)-NOT CALLED—91%: In the vast majority of cases-479 (91%) emergency medical services were not called following medication ingestion, and in no instance were they called for purposes of intervention.

C)-CALLED FOR OTHER REASONS: Those who called emergency medical services after ingesting a lethal dose of medication, but not for the reasons of intervention, were 4 in number (>1%). The explanation set forth by the Oregon Public Health Division for this statistic was as follows: "Calls included three to pronounce death and one to help a patient who had fallen."

§3.10)-GENDER
A)-TABLE-10

GENDER

	1998-2010 (N-525)	1998-2010 %	national %	Oregon %
Male	282	53.71	50.7	49.6
Female	243	46.29	49.3	50.4
totals	*525*	*100.00*	*100.0*	*100.0*

National and Oregon information from U.S. Census [www.census.gov]

The gender of the 525 ODWDA patients were almost evenly divided between men-282 patients—(54%), and women-243 patients—(46%) and were approximately the same as the national and Oregon census. The Washington experience was virtually the same as men—(52%) and women—(48%).

§3.11)-AGE
A)-TABLE-11

AGE

	1998-2010 (N-525)	1998-2010 %
18-34 (youngest—25)	6	1.14
35-44	13	2.48
45-54	39	7.43
55-64	107	20.38
65-74	146	27.81
75-84	151	28.76
85+	63	12.00
totals	*525*	*100.00*
Median years (range)	71 (25-96)	

As would be expected, over half-297 patients—(57%) of the 525 ODWDA patients were aged 65-84, with 63 patients—(12%) aged 85 and older. Only 6 patients—(1%) were in the range of 18-34 (with the youngest being 25), and another 13 patients—(2%) were in the range of 35-44. The median (mid-point) was 71 years calculated from a range of 25-96.

In Washington, the percentage of the patients in the 65-84 age classification was an almost identical 57%, but with a higher age range of 48-99.

§3.12)-EDUCATION
A)-TABLE-12

EDUCATION

	1998-2010 (N-525)	1998-2010 %	national %	Oregon %
Less than high school	37	7.05		
High school graduate	130	24.76		
Some college	125	23.81		
Baccalaureate or higher	231	44.00	24.4	25.1
Unknown	2	0.38		
totals	525	100.00		

National and Oregon information from U.S. Census [www.census.gov]

As far as education was concerned, only 37 patients—(7%) did not graduate from high school, 130 patients—(25%) were high school graduates, 125 patients—(24%) had some college, and 231 patients—(44%) had baccalaureate degrees or higher.

With the national and Oregon average of persons graduating college at 24% and 25% respectively, the Oregon Act patients were considerably more educated at 44%. So too were the Washington patients at 42%.

§3.13)-MARITAL STATUS
A)-TABLE-13
MARITAL STATUS

	1998-2010	1998-2010
	(N-525)	%
Married	245	46.67
Widowed	115	21.90
Never Married	42	8.00
Divorced	123	23.43
totals	525	100.00

The marital status of the 525 ODWDA population was as follows: 245 patient—(47%) were married at the time of their death, 115 patients—(22%) were widowed, 42 patients—(8%) were never married, and 123 patients—(23%) were divorced.

The Washington statistics were similar: married—(49%), widowed—(27%), never married—(6%), and divorced—(18%).

§3.14)-RACE
A)-TABLE-14
RACE

	1998-2010	1998-2010	national	Oregon
	(N-525)	%		
White	514	97.90	79.6	89.8
Asian	7	1.33	4.6	3.7
American Indian	1	0.19	1.0	1.6
African American	1	0.19	12.9	2.0
Hispanic	2	0.38	15.8	11.2
Other	0	0.00		
totals	525	100.00		

National and Oregon information from U.S. Census [www.census.gov]

The race of the 525 ODWDA patients was virtually all white-514 patients—(98%). This number is higher than both the nation—80% and Oregon—90%, but of course it is only Oregon that is relevant because the ODWDA only applies to Oregon Residents.

Because 98 percent of the patients were white, there were not many patients that fit into the minority categories: 7 patients—(1%) were Asian, one each (<1%) American Indian and African American, and 2 patients (<1%) were Hispanic. The Hispanic number of just 2 patients (<1%) was grossly underrepresented from an Oregon population of 11 percent.

The underrepresentation of minorities in the Oregon Death with Dignity Act runs contra to some who feared that minorities would be represented in a disproportionately high level.

Just as Oregon had 98% white, Washington had 96%.

§3.15)-PARTICIPATING PHYSICIANS

Unfortunately, the Oregon Public Health Division does not provide regular statistics as to the number of different physicians who participate in the Oregon Death with Dignity Act. Some numbers appear in the various press release issued by the division.

In the case of the first ten patients there were nine different attending physicians. [Oregon Press Release 8/18/98]

In 2005, thirty-nine physicians wrote a total of 64 prescriptions for lethal doses of medication. [Oregon Press Release 3/9/06]

Washington also had a diverse number of participating physicians: 68 for 119 patients.

PART-II
WASHINGTON DEATH WITH DIGNITY ACT

To be read by residents of the state of Washington.

CHAPTER-FOUR
QUALIFIED PATIENT

WASHINGTON DEATH WITH DIGNITY ACT
("WDWDA") or ("Washington Act")

NOTE: The first three chapters of this book dealt with the Oregon Death with Dignity Act. Chapters four, five and six are devoted to the Washington Death with Dignity Act.

Both Acts were the result of voters' referendum: the Oregon Act in 1994, and the Washington Act in 2008. The content of the Washington Act is virtually identical to that of the Oregon Act, except for a few terms, statutory citations and statistics.

TABLE OF CONTENTS

NOTE: This chapter/book does not contain legal or medical advice, which can only be obtained from the reader's personal attorney or physician.

WASHINGTON DEATH WITH DIGNITY ACT (WDWDA)

§4.01)-"QUALIFIED PATIENT"

ONLY A "QUALIFIED PATIENT" IS ELIGIBLE TO RECEIVE THE BENEFITS OF THE WASHINGTON DEATH WITH DIGNITY ACT.

The Washington Death with Dignity Act ("WDWDA") or the ("Washington Act") limits it applicability to a "qualified patient":

> **"Qualified patient"** means a <u>competent</u> <u>adult</u> who is a <u>resident of Washington</u> state and has satisfied the requirements of this chapter in order to obtain a prescription for medication that the qualified patient may self-administer to end his or her life in a humane and dignified manner.
>
> [WDWDA RCW 70.245.010(11) (emphasis supplied)]

§4.02)-"ADULT"—18 YEARS OLD OR OLDER

ONLY AN "ADULT", 18 YEARS OLD OR OLDER CAN BE A QUALIFIED PATIENT.

A patient must be an adult defined as an individual who is eighteen years of age or older. [WDWDA RCW 70.245.010(1)]

In the two year history of the Washington Act, from 2009-2010, out of 119 patients none were in the age groups of 18-34 or 35-44, with the youngest patient being 48. In the thirteen year history of the Oregon Act, from 1998-2010, there were 6 patients in the 18-34 age group, with the youngest being 25.

§4.03)-"RESIDENCY REQUIREMENT"

ONLY A "RESIDENT" OF THE STATE OF WASHINGTON CAN MAKE A REQUEST UNDER THE ACT.

While a qualified patient, as quoted above, must be a resident of Washington, the Act goes on to be even more emphatic:

> **Residency requirement** Only requests made by Washington state residents under this chapter may be granted.
>
> [WDWDA RCW 70.245.130]

A)-WASHINGTON DEFINITION OF RESIDENT: The most common area in which the concept of residency is at issue is in the realm of taxation. As posted on the website of the Washington State's Department of Revenue:

Washington State residency definition:

The state of Washington does not have a personal or corporate income tax. Persons are considered residents of this state for sales and use tax purposes if they take any <u>actions which indicate that they intend to live in this state on more than a temporary or transient basis</u>. A person may be considered a resident of this state even though the person is a resident of another state. The Department of Revenue presumes that a person is a resident of this state if he or she does any of the following:

> Maintains a residence in Washington for personal use;
> Is registered to vote in this state;
> Uses a Washington address for federal or state taxes;
> Has a Washington State driver's license.

[http://dor.wa.gov/content/contactus/con_residdef.aspx
(emphasis supplied) 6/20/11]

B)-"FACTORS" DEMONSTRATING RESIDENCY: Under the Washington Act, the following constitute what the Act referred to as "factors demonstrating Washington state residency":

> **Residency requirement.**
> … Factors demonstrating Washington state residency include but are not limited to:
> (1) Possession of an **Washington state driver's license**;
> (2) **Registration to vote** in Washington state; or
> (3) Evidence that the person **owns or leases property** in Washington state.
>
> [WDWDA RCW 70.245.130]

C)-ADDITIONAL PROOFS: The above set forth "factors" are proceeded by the phrase "include but are not limited to." The meaning of this term is that the three enunciated factors are only examples, and satisfying all three of these factors is not required for a determination of Washington residency, but each would be of primary importance.

The Washington State Department of Revenue's definition of residency highlights: "actions which indicate that they intend to live in this state on more than a temporary or transient basis;" and "maintains a residence in Washington for personal use." Proofs incident to the ownership of a house or a lease on an apartment, may include such items as: a gas/electric account, a land line telephone contract, TV and computer service, the purchase of furniture, and local bank and brokerage accounts.

The Washington Division of Motor Vehicles, in addition to a driver's license, also requires the registration of automobiles. Thus, a registration of a patient's automobile is another proof of residency.

D)-NO RESIDENCY PERIOD: The Washington Act is silent as to any required residency period. Of course, the longer a qualified patient has resided in the State of Washington, the easier it is to prove residency.

E)-LONG TERM PHYSICIAN-PATIENT RELATIONSHIP: The best single factor in establishing Washington residency is a long term relationship between the physician and patient.

In the two year history of the Washington Act, from 2009-2010, out of 119 patients the duration of the patient-physician relationship showed 57—(51%) in the category of 3-weeks to 24 weeks. In the thirteen year history of the Oregon Act, from 1998-2010, the median duration of the patient-physician relationship was 10 weeks with the shortest being less than a week.

F)-PHYSICIAN'S DOCUMENT RESPONSIBILITY: Because the Washington Act requires residency, and because the attending physician is responsible for obtaining proof of residency from the patient, all forms of proof should be assembled prior to a first meeting with the physician.

§4.04)-"COMPETENT"

A QUALIFIED PATIENT MUST BE "COMPETENT" OF HAVING THE ABILITY TO MAKE AND COMMUNICATE HEALTH CARE DECISIONS.

Under the Washington Act a patient must be "competent" of communicating his or her health care decisions.

> **"Competent"** means that, in the opinion of a court or in the opinion of the patient's attending physician or consulting physician, psychiatrist, or psychologist, a patient has the ability to make and communicate an informed decision to health care providers, including communication through persons familiar with the patient's manner of communicating if those persons are available.
>
> [WDWDA RCW 70.245.010(3) (emphasis supplied)]

A short observation re nomenclature: the Washington Act uses the term "competent," whereas the Oregon Act employs the term "capable." There is no distinction between these two terms.

A)-ABILITY TO COMMUNICATE: In those cases where a patient cannot communicate directly with the physician because of speech impediments or other condition, such communications can be accomplished through a "person[] familiar with the patient's manner of communicating."

B)-ABILITY TO UNDERSTAND: In addition to the requirement that a patient must be able to communicate health care decisions, a further requirement is that the patient must be able to understand his/her medical "diagnosis and prognosis." This requirement originated within the context of a consulting physician's responsebility to provide a second opinion based on these factors. [WDWDA, RCW 70.245.010(4)]

C)-VOLUNTARY DECISION: The Washington Act is concerned with the risk of a patient making a decision as a result of undue influence. Thus, under the title "Written request for medication," there is the provision that the patient: "has voluntarily expressed his or her wish to die…." [WDWDA, RCW 70.245.020(1)]

§4.05)-"INFORMED DECISION"

AN "INFORMED DECISION" IS MORE THAN "INFORMED CONSENT".

A patient must be capable of making an "informed decision." Under the Washington Act that term is defined as follows:

"Informed decision"

means a decision by a qualified patient, to request and obtain a prescription for medication that the qualified patient may self-administer to end his or her life in a humane and dignified manner, that is based on an appreciation of the relevant facts and after being fully informed by the attending physician of:

(a) His or her medical diagnosis;

(b) His or her prognosis;

(c) The potential risks associated with taking the medication to be prescribed;

(d) The probable result of taking the medication to be prescribed; and

(e) The feasible alternatives including, but not limited to, comfort care, hospice care, and pain control.

[WDWDA RCW 70.245.010(7)]

A)-INFORMED CONSENT: For the purposes of a patient making an "informed consent" a physician must provide a general description of the nature of the procedure along with risks and alternatives. The physician must then ask the patient if he/she has any questions.

B)-INFORMED DECISION: The burden on the physician in the case of an informed decision is greater than "informed consent." In addition to providing a general description, the physician <u>must</u> also inform the patient of those details that would have been supplied upon request in the instance of an informed consent. In other words, the physician has no choice but to provide the details whether or not the patient initiates the request.

§4.06)-TERMINAL DISEASE

A TERMINAL DISEASE IS ONE THAT IS INCURABLE, IRREVERSIBLE AND WILL PRODUCE DEATH WITH-IN SIX MONTHS.

To be a qualified patient he/she must have a terminal disease:

> **Written request for medication.**
> An adult who is competent, is a resident of Washington state, and has been determined by the attending physician and consulting physician to be <u>suffering from a</u> **terminal disease**....
> [WDWDA RCW 70.245.020(1) (emphasis supplied)]

At other places in the Washington Act the term "illness" is used instead of the term "disease," without distinction.

A)-TERMINAL DISEASE-DEFINED: The Washington Act defines terminal disease as a period of time:

> **"Terminal disease"** means an **incurable** and **irreversible** disease that has been medically confirmed and will, within reasonable medical judgment, produce **death within six months**.
> [WDWDA RCW 70.245.010(13) (emphasis supplied)]

B)-PREDICTING SIX MONTH PERIOD: As set forth above, one element in the definition of a terminal disease is that it will "produce death within six months." This requirement is couched in terms of a "reasonable medical judgment." It can be noted that the six month element is also applicable for hospice care:

> In the United States, people with Medicare (and most other private insurance) can receive hospice care if their doctor believes that they most likely have less than 6 months to live if their illness runs a normal or typical course. … If the patient lives longer … the doctor and the hospice team will re-certify that the patient is terminally ill and that hospice services are appropriate. There is no end to the hospice benefit under Medicare if the patient continues to meet the "expected within the next 6 months" criteria.
>
> [http://www.eldercareteam.com/public/639.cfm]

§4.07)-SOUND JUDGEMENT

TO BE A QUALIFIED PATIENT, ONE MUST NOT BE SUFFERING FROM A PSYCHIATRIC OR PSYCHOLOGICAL DISORDER OR DEPRESSION CAUSING IMPAIRED JUDGMENT.

A principal safeguard in the Washington Death with Dignity Act is the requirement that the patient have sound judgment, as phrased in the negative: "the patient is not suffering from a psychiatric or psychological disorder or depression causing impaired judgment." Note that the operative phrase is "impaired judgment." Thus, it is to be expected that patients facing the end of their lives from terminal diseases, with no more than six months to live, with many in extreme pain, will be depressed. But it is only depression which causes "impaired judgment" that disqualifies a patient.

> **Counseling referral.**
> If, in the opinion of the attending physician or the consulting physician, a patient may be suffering from a <u>psychiatric or psychological disorder or depression causing impaired judgment</u>, either physician shall refer the patient for counseling. Medication to end a patient's life in a humane and dignified manner shall not be prescribed until the person performing the counseling determines that the patient is not suffering from a psychiatric or psychological disorder or depression causing impaired judgment.
>
> [WDWDA RCW 70.245.060 (emphasis supplied)]

It should be noted that "impaired judgment," as used in the Washington Act, is not equivalent to the concept of lack of testamentary capacity.

§4.08)-"COUNSELING"

<u>COUNSELING MEANS BEING SEEN BY A STATE LICENSED PSYCHIATRIST OR PSYCHOLOGIST TO DETERMINE IF THE PATIENT IS CAPABLE.</u>

The previous section, dealing with the requirement for a sound mind, discussed the need for a counseling referral in the event that a physician has concluded that a patient "may" be "suffering from a psychiatric or psychological disorder or depression causing impaired judgment." As to what constitutes counseling, the Washington Act states:

> **"Counseling"** means <u>one or more consultations</u> as necessary between a <u>state licensed psychiatrist or psychologist</u> and a patient for the purpose of determining that the patient is competent and not suffering from a psychiatric or psychological disorder or depression causing impaired judgment.
>
> [WDWDA RCW 70.245.010(5) (emphasis supplied)]

A)-STATE LICENSED PROFESSIONALS: Only psychiatrists and psychologists licensed in the State of Washington are permitted to conduct the counseling evaluations under the Washington Act.

B)-COUNSELING STATISTIC

The Washington Act's experience over the two year period it was in effect (2009-2010) has seen only 5 of its patients—4%) being referred for evaluation

This five percent only deals with this 119 population, and does not reflect how many may have been referred to counseling and found to have been not of sound mind, and thus were not qualified patients and therefore could not participate in the program.

In the first thirteen years (1998-2010) that the Oregon Act was in effect, of the 525 patients that were provided with life ending medications, 39—(7%) had first been referred to counseling.

§4.09)-NON-QUALIFYING SOLELY AGE OR DISABILITY

NO PERSON SHALL QUALIFY ... SOLELY BE-CAUSE OF AGE OR DISABILITY

As stated earlier in the chapter, one of the requirements to be a qualified patient is having a terminal disease.

To emphasize this point, the Washington Act states that no one can become a qualified patient solely because of age or disability.

> A person does not qualify ... solely because of age or disability.
>
> [WDWDA RCW 70.245.020(2)]

[page left blank]

CHAPTER-FIVE
PROCEDURES

WASHINGTON DEATH WITH DIGNITY ACT ("WDWDA") or ("WASHINGTON ACT")

TABLE OF CONTENTS

NOTE: This chapter/book does not contain legal or medical advice, which can only be obtained from the reader's personal attorney or physician.

§5.01)-QUALIFIED PATIENT

AS SET FORTH IN CHAPTER-FOUR OF THIS BOOK, A "QUALIFIED PATIENT" IS: 1)-AN ADULT; 2)-COMPETENT; 3)-WASHINGTON RESIDENT; 4)-SUFFERING FROM A TERMINAL DISEASE; 5)-WITH LESS THAN SIX MONTHS TO LIVE.

The Washington Death with Dignity Act is only available to a "qualified patient." Chapter-Four of this book details the required characteristics in order to achieve the classification of a qualified patient.

§5.02)-THREE REQUESTS

IN ORDER TO RECEIVE A PRESCRIPTION FOR MEDICATION TO END LIFE, A PATIENT MUST MAKE THREE REQUESTS: TWO ORALLY AND ONE IN WRITING.

The necessity of making three requests according to the Washington Death with Dignity Act is stated as follows:

Written and oral requests.
To receive a prescription for medication that the qualified patient may self-administer to end his or her life in a humane and dignified manner, a qualified patient shall have made <u>an oral request</u> and <u>a written request</u>, and reiterate the oral request to his or her attending physician at least fifteen days after making the initial oral request. At the time the qualified patient makes his or her <u>second oral request</u>, the attending physician shall offer the qualified patient an opportunity to rescind the request.

[WDWDA RCW 70.245.090 (emphasis supplied)]

A)-INITIAL ORAL REQUEST: To start the process under the Washington Act, a qualified patient must make an initial oral request for a prescription for medication to end his or her life in a humane and dignified manner.

B)-WRITTEN REQUEST: After making the initial oral request, the qualified patient must make a written request in the form prescribed under the Act, and set forth later in this chapter.

C)-SECOND ORAL REQUEST: The qualified patient must make a second oral request.

D)-WAITING PERIODS: The Washington Act provides two waiting periods:

> **Waiting periods.**
>
> (1) At least <u>fifteen days</u> shall elapse between the patient's initial oral request and the writing of a prescription under this chapter.
>
> (2) At least <u>forty-eight hours</u> shall elapse between the date the patient signs the written request and the writing of a prescription under this chapter.
>
> [WDWDA RCW 70.245.110 (emphasis supplied)]

E)-15 DAY PROCESS: The fastest that the system can work is 15 days using the following timing:

> first)-make the initial oral request on day-one;
>
> second)-make the written request within the next thirteen days; and
>
> third)-make the second oral request fifteen days after the first oral request.

§5.03)-RIGHT TO RESCIND

<u>A PATIENT MAY ALWAYS RESCIND HIS/HER REQUEST FOR MEDICATION AND THE PHYSICIAN MUST PROVIDE THE OPPORTUNITY.</u>

One of the safeguards in the Washington Act is the requirement that the physician give the patient the right to rescind upon receiving the second oral request, and that the patient always has the right to rescind thereafter. If any time elapses between the second oral request and the writing of the prescription, the physician must offer the qualified patient another opportunity to rescind.

> **Right to rescind request.**
> A patient may rescind his or her request at any time and in any manner without regard to his or her mental state. No prescription for medication under this chapter may be written without the attending physician offering the qualified patient an opportunity to rescind the request.
>
> [WDWDA RCW 70.245.100 (emphasis supplied)]

§5.04)-CONSULTING PHYSICIAN

TWO PHYSICIANS MUST VERIFY THE TERMINAL DISEASE OF THE QUALIFIED PATIENT: FIRST THE ATTENDING PHYSICIAN AND THEN A CONSULTING PHYSICIAN.

A safeguard of the Washington Act is the requirement that the opinion of the attending physician be backed up by a second physician—called the consulting physician

> **Consulting physician confirmation.**
> Before a patient is qualified under this chapter, a consulting physician shall examine the patient and his or her relevant medical records and confirm, in writing, the attending physician's diagnosis that the patient is suffering from a terminal disease, and verify that the patient is competent, is acting voluntarily, and has made an informed decision.
>
> [WDWDA RCW 70.245.050]

§5.05)-FORM OF WRITTEN REQUEST

A WRITTEN REQUEST MUST BE IN THE FORM PROVIDED IN THE ACT, AND CONTAIN TWO WITNESSES.

The Washington Act contains a form that must be followed in order for a qualified patient to make a written request:

**REQUEST FOR MEDICATION
TO END MY LIFE IN A HUMANE
AND DIGNIFIED MANNER**

I,. . . . ., am an adult of sound mind.

I am suffering from . . . ., which my attending physician has determined is a terminal disease and which has been medically confirmed by a consulting physician.

I have been fully informed of my diagnosis, prognosis, the nature of medication to be prescribed and potential associated risks, the expected result, and the feasible alternatives, including comfort care, hospice care, and pain control.

I request that my attending physician prescribe medication that I may self-administer to end my life in a humane and dignified manner and to contact any pharmacist to fill the prescription.

INITIAL ONE:

. . . . . I have informed my family of my decision and taken their opinions into consideration.

. . . . . I have decided not to inform my family of my decision.

. . . . . I have no family to inform of my decision.

I understand that I have the right to rescind this request at any time.

I understand the full import of this request and I expect to die when I take the medication to be prescribed. I further understand that although most deaths occur

---

> within three hours, my death may take longer and my physician has counseled me about this possibility.
>
> I make this request voluntarily and without reservation, and I accept full moral responsibility for my actions.
>
> Signed:. . . . .
>
> Dated:. . . . .
>
> [WDWDA RCW 70.245.220]

A)-AFTER CONSULTING PHYSICIAN: Note that the written request cannot be prepared until after a consulting physician has confirmed the presence of the terminal disease. Thus, to keep the waiting periods as short as possible it is important to obtain the opinion of the consulting physician as soon as possible.

B)-TWO WITNESSES—ONE INDEPENDENT: The written request must be witnessed by two witnesses, and at least one must be independent:

> **Form of the written request.**
>
> (1) A valid request for medication under this chapter shall be in substantially the form described in RCW 70.245.220, signed and dated by the patient and witnessed by at least two individuals who, in the presence of the patient, attest that to the best of their knowledge and belief the patient is competent, acting voluntarily, and is not being coerced to sign the request.
>
> (2) One of the witnesses shall be a person who is not:
>
> (a) A relative of the patient by blood, marriage, or adoption;
>
> (b) A person who at the time the request is signed would be entitled to any portion of the estate of the qualified patient upon death under any will or by operation of law; or

> (c) An owner, operator, or employee of a health care facility where the qualified patient is receiving medical treatment or is a resident.
>
> (3) The patient's attending physician at the time the request is signed shall not be a witness.
>
> [WDWDA RCW 70.245.030]

C)-LONG TERM CARE FACILITY: If the patient is in a long term care facility one of the two witnesses must be from that facility:

> If the patient is a patient in a long-term care facility at the time the written request is made, one of the witnesses shall be an individual designated by the facility and having the qualifications specified by the department of health by rule.
>
> [WDWDA RCW 70.245.030(4)]

§5.06)-THE WDWDA IS NOT ASSISTED-SUICIDE

THE WASHINGTON DEATH WITH DIGNITY ACT DOES NOT CONSTITUTE SUICIDE, ASSISTED SUICIDE, MERCY KILLING OR HOMICIDE.

The Washington Death with Dignity Act is crystal clear that the patient's actions, and those of the physicians, do not constitute suicide, assisted suicide, mercy killing or homicide:

> **References to practices under this chapter.**
> …. Actions taken in accordance with this chapter do not, for any purpose, constitute suicide, assisted suicide, mercy killing, or homicide, under the law. State reports shall not refer to practice under this chapter as "suicide" or "assisted suicide." Consistent with [this Act] state reports shall refer to practice under this chapter as obtaining and self-administering life-ending medication.
>
> [WDWDA RCW 70.245.180(1)]

§5.07)-EUTHANASIA IS HOMICIDE

ACTIONS TAKEN BY A PHYSICIAN OUTSIDE THE SPECIFIC PROVISIONS OF THE WASHINGTON DEATH WITH DIGNITY ACT CAN CONSTITUTE HOMICIDE.

As stated above, a physician's actions under the WDWDA do not constitute assisted suicide, mercy killing or homicide. But, actions by a physician outside the Act can constitute homicide. An example of actions that can constitute homicide can be found in the following subsection on euthanasia.

A)-HOMICIDE: Under Washington law, as well as the law in all fifty states, euthanasia is homicide.

References to practices under this chapter.
Nothing in this chapter authorizes a physician or any other person to end a patient's life by lethal injection, mercy killing, or active euthanasia.

[WDWDA RCW 70.245.180(1)]

B)-EUTHANASIA: The all important distinction between "physician-assisted death"—specifically made legal under the Washington Death with Dignity Act, and "euthanasia"— specifically excluded from the Act and thus presumably prosecutable as homicide, revolves around the issue of who administers the medication. When the patient self-administers the medication—physician-assisted death; when the physician or other individual administers the medication—homicide.

C)-ADMINISTERS MEDICATION: It is easy to differentiate between, on the one hand, a patient on his/her own drinking the medication, and on the other hand a physician providing a lethal injection. What is not so easy to discern is when allowable assistance become unlawful administration. That is the subject of the next section.

§5.08)-SELF ADMINISTRATION AND ASSISTANCE

UNDER THE WASHINGTON DEATH WITH DIGNITY ACT A PATIENT MUST SELF-ADMINISTER THE MEDICATION TO END HIS/HER LIFE.

A patient, and only the patient, must self-administer the medication to end his/her life. As stated in the written request for the medication:

> **Request for medication.**
> I understand the full import of this request and I expect to die when I take the medication to be prescribed.
> [WDWDA RCW 70.245.220]

A)-ASSISTANCE: The Washington Death with Dignity Act does not provide guidance as to what actions on the part of another person (physician, healthcare provider, or other individual) will be construed as allowable assistance and what will constitute unlawful administration.

The history of Dr. Jack Kevorkian is instructive. On numerous occasions Dr. Kevorkian was put on trial for physician-assisted suicide, only to be acquitted each time. In all these instances, he mixed a lethal dose of medication in a machine, attached the machine to the patient, and then let the patient push the final button that delivered the medication and brought about death. Thus, in the final instance, the patient always self-administered the lethal dose of medication.

Then, Dr. Kevorkian decided to push the envelope, by being the individual that actually pushed the button without assistance from the patient. He was then prosecuted and convicted of homicide.

The lesson, as it pertains to the Washington Death with Dignity Act, is that individuals can assist in providing some form of very limited physical assistance, but the patient must remain in complete control of the decision, timing and actually taking the lethal dose of medication. Control over the decision and the timing are easy to determine. The action of taking the medication is more difficult to measure. As long as the patient has the capacity to swallow, it might be allowable for an individual to hold the glass up to the patient's mouth or other types of very limited physical assistance.

B)-DEATH AT HOME WITHOUT A PHYSICIAN: As will be more fully seen in Chapter-Six Statistics, (92%) chose to die at home, and in those instances the prescribing physician was present in only 6 percent of the time. As a practical matter it might be easier for a member of the patient's immediate family to provide required assistance.

§5.09)-FAMILY NOTIFICATION

IT IS RECOMMENDED THAT A PATIENT NOTIFY NEXT OF KIN, BUT FAILURE TO DO SO MAY NOT BE HELD AGAINST THE PATIENT.

The Washington Act recommends that a patient notify his/her family of the decision, but the patient cannot be penalized for declining the recommendation.

> **Notification of next of kin.**
> The attending physician shall recommend that the patient notify the next of kin of his or her request for medication under this chapter. A patient who declines or is unable to notify next of kin shall not have his or her request denied for that reason.
>
> [WDWDA RCW 70.245.080]

§5.10)-WILLS, CONTRACTS AND STATUTES

NO PROVISION IN ANY WILL, CONTRACT OR OTHER AGREEMENT SHALL AFFECT THE USE OF THE WASHINGTON DEATH WITH DIGNITY ACT.

The Washington Act is sacrosanct in that it cannot be affected by contrary provisions in wills, contracts and other agreements. Thus, for example, if a contract states that it will be invalid if a contracting party utilizes the Washington Death with Dignity Act, said provision would be null and void.

Effect on construction of wills, contracts and statutes.

(1) Any provision in a contract, will, or other agreement, whether written or oral, to the extent the provision would affect whether a person may make or rescind a request for medication to end his or her life in a humane and dignified manner, is not valid.

(2) Any obligation owing under any currently existing contract shall not be conditioned or affected by the making or rescinding of a request, by a person, for medication to end his or her life in a humane and dignified manner.

[WDWDA RCW 70.245.160]

---

§5.11)-INSURANCE AND ANNUITY POLICIES

THE USE OF THE WASHINGTON DEATH WITH DIGNITY DOES NOT HAVE ANY EFFECT ON INSURANCE POLICIES.

The employment of the Washington Act to bring about the death of an insured cannot be used by an insurance company to negate the insurance policy's coverage. For example, it would seem to be the case that an insurance policy with a provision negating coverage if the insured commits suicide within the first one or two years could not be used if the insured terminates his/her own life pursuant to the Washington Act.

Insurance or annuity policies.
The sale, procurement, or issuance of any life, health, or accident insurance or annuity policy or the rate charged for any policy shall not be conditioned upon or affected

---

by the making or rescinding of a request, by a person, for medication that the patient may self-administer to end his or her life in a humane and dignified manner. A qualified patient's act of ingesting medication to end his or her life in a humane and dignified manner shall not have an effect upon a life, health, or accident insurance or annuity policy.

[WDWDA RCW 70.245.170]

§5.12)-IMMUNITIES AND LIABILITIES

A PHYSICIAN OR OTHER INDIVIDUAL TAKING ACTIONS IN ACCORDANCE WITH THE WASHINGTON ACT IS IMMUNE FROM CIVIL OR CRIMINAL LIABILITY.

While the Washington Act specifies that it does not constitute "suicide, assisted suicide, mercy killing or homicide," the Act goes on to specify that actions taken under the Act cannot be the basis for civil or criminal liability. Thus, physicians and other individuals are secure from a lawsuit brought by an aggrieved relative of the patient for negligence for participation, and can prevail over a prosecution for homicide or other battery. These immunities can be claimed for those "participating in good faith compliance.

Immunities; ... permissible sanctions.
Except as provided in [the WDWDA]:
A person shall not be subject to civil or criminal liability or professional disciplinary action for participating in good faith compliance with this chapter. This includes being present when a qualified patient takes the prescribed medication to end his or her life in a humane and dignified manner;
....
  A patient's request for or provision by an attending physician of medication in good faith compliance with this chapter does not constitute neglect for any purpose of

law or provide the sole basis for the appointment of a guardian or conservator;

[WDWDA RCW 70.245.190(1)(a) and (1)(c)]

§5.13)-CONSCIENTIOUS OBJECTION

NO ONE IS FORCED TO PARTICIPATE IN THE WASHINGTON DEATH WITH DIGNITY ACT. THOSE WITH A CONSCIENTIOUS OBJECTION MAY OBSTAIN WITHOUT PENALTY.

There are those who oppose the Washington Death with Dignity Act on moral grounds and under no circumstances would agree to participate in providing qualified patients with lethal doses of medication to end their lives. These individuals can be physicians, psychiatrists, psychologists, and any other health care provider. These individuals are conscientious objectors, and have the absolute right to abstain from participation.

Immunities; basis for prohibiting health care provider from participation; notification; permissible sanctions.

A professional organization or association, or health care provider, may not subject a person to censure, discipline, suspension, loss of license, loss of privileges, loss of membership, or other penalty for participating or refusing to participate in good faith compliance with [the WDWDA].

[WDWDA RCW 70.245.190(1)(b)]

§5.14)-DEATH IN A PUBLIC PLACE PROHIBITED
THE WASHINGTON DEATH WITH DIGNITY ACT IMPOSES PENALTIES FOR PATIENTS WHO CHOOSE TO DIE IN A PUBLIC PLACE.

The Washington Act provides penalties against those patients who terminate their lives in a public place:

> **Claims by governmental entity for costs incurred.**
> Any governmental entity that incurs costs resulting from a person terminating his or her life under this chapter in a public place has a claim against the estate of the person to recover such costs and reasonable attorneys' fees related to enforcing the claim.
>
> [WDWDA RCW 70.245.210]

§5.15)-CRIMINAL PENALTIES

IT IS A CLASS-A FELONY TO WILLFULLY ALTER, FORGE, CONCEAL OR DESTROY A DOCUMENT CREATED PURSUANT TO THE WASHINGTON DEATH WITH DIGNITY ACT.

A Class A Felony in the State of Washington is punishable by a maximum sentence of life in prison and a $50,000 fine. The "penalties" section in the Washington Death with Dignity Act specified the following:

> **Penalties.**
> (1) A person who without authorization of the patient willfully alters or forges a request for medication or conceals or destroys a rescission of that request with the intent or effect of causing the patient's death is guilty of a class A felony.
> (2) A person who coerces or exerts undue influence on a patient to request medication to end the patient's life, or to destroy a rescission of a request, is guilty of a class A felony.
> (3) This chapter does not limit further liability for civil damages resulting from other negligent conduct or intentional misconduct by any person.
> (4) The penalties in this chapter do not preclude criminal penalties applicable under other law for conduct that is inconsistent with this chapter.
>
> [WDWDA RCW 70.245.200]

§5.16)-INITIATING THE CONVERSATION

AS BETWEEN THE PATIENT AND THE PHYSICIAN, IT IS THE PATIENT'S RESPONSIBILITY TO INITIATE THE CONVERSATION REGARDING THE WASHINGTON DEATH WITH DIGNITY ACT.

A patient has many end-of-life options, one of which is the Washington Death with Dignity Act. Awareness of this option is the problem. As between the patient and the physician it might be the patient's responsibility to initiate the discussion.

A physician might initiate the conversation with his/her patient regarding the Oregon Death with Dignity Act. But then again, the physician might refrain from initiating this discussion because of the appearance of undue influence.

§5.17)-ATTENDING PHYSICIAN RESPONSIBILITIES

THE ATTENDING PHYSICIAN HAS THE RESPONSIBILITY OF INSURING COMPLIANCE WITH ALL THE PROVISIONS OF THE WASHINGTON DEATH WITH DIGNITY ACT

A separate section of the Washington Act is entitled "Attending physician responsibilities." In essence, the attending physician is the Act's administrator.

Set forth below is the section regarding the attending physician's responsibilities, with captions added as shown in brackets "[]."

Attending physician responsibilities.
    (1) The attending physician shall:
[INITIAL DETERMINATION] (a) Make the initial determination of whether a patient has a terminal disease, is competent, and has made the request voluntarily;

[WASHINGTON RESIDENCY] (b) Request that the patient demonstrate Washington state residency …;

[INFORMED DECISION] (c) To ensure that the patient is making an informed decision, inform the patient of: (i) His or her medical diagnosis; (ii) His or her prognosis; (iii) The potential risks associated with taking the medication to be prescribed; (iv) The probable result of taking the medication to be prescribed; and v) The feasible alternatives including, but not limited to, comfort care, hospice care, and pain control;

[CONSULTING PHYSICIAN] (d) Refer the patient to a consulting physician for medical confirmation of the diagnosis, and for a determination that the patient is competent and acting voluntarily;

[COUNSELING] (e) Refer the patient for counseling if appropriate …;

[FAMILY NOTIFICATION] (f) Recommend that the patient notify next of kin;

[PRESENCE OF ANOTHER PERSON] (g) Counsel the patient about the importance of having another person present when the patient takes the medication prescribed …

[PUBLIC PLACE] and of not taking the medication in a public place;

[OFFER TO RESCIND] (h) Inform the patient that he or she has an opportunity to rescind the request at any time and in any manner, and offer the patient an opportunity to rescind at the end of the fifteen-day waiting period …;

[INFORMED DECISION] (i) Verify, immediately before writing the prescription for medication under this chapter, that the patient is making an informed decision;

[MEDICAL RECORDS] (j) Fulfill the medical record documentation requirements…; (k) Ensure that all appropriate steps are carried out in accordance with this chapter before writing a prescription for medication to enable a qualified patient to end his or her life in a humane and dignified manner; and

[DISPENSING MEDICATIONS] (l)(i) Dispense medications directly, including ancillary medications intended to facilitate the desired effect to minimize the patient's discomfort, if the attending physician is authorized under statute and rule to dispense and has a current drug enforcement administration certificate; or

[PHARMACIST] (ii) With the patient's written consent:

(A) Contact a pharmacist and inform the pharmacist of the prescription; and

(B) Deliver the written prescription personally, by mail or facsimile to the pharmacist, who will dispense the medications directly to either the patient, the attending physician, or an expressly identified agent of the patient. Medications dispensed pursuant to this subsection shall not be dispensed by mail or other form of courier.

[DEATH CERTIFICATE] (2) The attending physician may sign the patient's death certificate which shall list the underlying terminal disease as the cause of death.

[WDWDA RCW 70.245.040 (brackets supplied)]

§5.18)-STATISTICES—CHAPTER SIX

The next chapter in this book discusses the statistical history of the Washington Death with Dignity Act.

CHAPTER-SIX
STATISTICS
2009-2010   2 YEARS   119 PATIENTS
WASHINGTON DEATH WITH DIGNITY ACT
("WDWDA") or ("Washington Act")

TABLE OF CONTENTS

NOTE: This chapter/book does not contain legal or medical advice, which can only be obtained from the reader's personal attorney or physician.

INTRODUCTION

WASHINGTON STATISTICS—("WDWDA"): As of the end of 2010, the State of Washington had two years' experience with the Washington Death with Dignity Act ("WDWDA") or simply the "Washington Act."

The Washington State Department of Health published a report entitled: "Washington State Department of Health 2010 Death with Dignity Act Report," which, while dealing with the years 2009 and 2010, included data from the documentation received by the Department of Health as of February 9, 2011.

The statistics derived from this report are summarized in the below text, and the detailed tables that follow.

STAND ALONE CHAPTER: This chapter is meant to stand alone, meaning that some material in the commentary is repeated at other places of this book.

OREGON STATISTICS—("ODWDA"): Frequent references will be made to statistics from the Oregon Death with Dignity Act ("ODWDA") or simply the "Oregon Act." Oregon was the first state to adopt a Death with Dignity Act in 1994, with prescriptions starting in 1998. The thirteen year history of the Oregon Act, from 1998 to 2010, consists of 525 patients who have died from ingesting medications prescribed under the ODWSA.

§6.01)-RESIDENCE REQUIREMENT
A)-TABLE-1

RESIDENCE

	2009-2010 (N-119)	2009-2010 %
West of the Cascades	112	94.12
East of the Cascades	7	5.88
totals	*119*	*100.00*

As can be seen, all 119 WDWDA patients resided in the State of Washington, as required under that state's act.

> **Residency requirement.**
> Only requests made by Washington state residents under
> this chapter may be granted.
>
> [WDWDA RCW 70.245.130]

B)-"FACTORS" DEMONSTRATING RESIDENCY: Under the Washington Act, the following constitute what the Act referred to as "factors demonstrating Washington state residency":

> **Residency requirement.**
> … Factors demonstrating Washington state residency
> include but are not limited to:
>   (1) Possession of an **Washington state driver's
> license**;
>   (2) **Registration to vote** in Washington state; or
>   (3) Evidence that the person **owns or leases property**
> in Washington state.
>
> [WDWDA RCW 70.245.130]

C)-DURATION OF PATIENT-PHYSICIAN RELATIONSHIP

As will be discussed at length in §6.06, the duration of the patient-physician relationship ranged from 3 weeks to 10 years in 2009, and from 3 weeks to 27 years in 2010.

Thus, if other evidence of residency can be established, a lengthy patient-physician relationship may not be required.

§6.02)-UNDERLYING ILLNESS
A)-TABLE-2: UNDERLYING ILLNESS

	2009-2010 (N-119)	2009-2010 %
Cancer	93	78.15
Neuro-degenerative disease (incl. ALS)	11	9.24
Respiratory disease (incl. COPD)	5	4.20
Heart disease	6	5.04
Other illnesses	4	3.36
totals	*119*	*100.00*

B)-CANCER—78%: By far and away the most numerous underlying illnesses in the 119 WDWDA population is cancer—93 patients—(78%).

The cancer deaths experienced under the Oregon Act mirror the above statistic for cancer—424 patients--(81%).

C)-NEURO-DEGENERATIVE DISEASE (incl. ALS)—9%: The next largest group is those with neuro-degenerative disease (including ALS, also known as Lou Gehrig's disease), 11-patients—(9%).

The above category under the Oregon Act is captioned: "amyotrophic lateral sclerosis (ALS), and constituted 42-patients—(8%).

D)-RESPIRATORY DISEASE—4%: The next category of illness is respiratory disease which includes COPD, effecting 5 patients—(4%).

E)-HEART DISEASE—5%: The fourth largest category of illness was heart disease, effecting 6 patients—(5%).

§6.03)-END OF LIFE CONCERNS
A)-TABLE-3
END OF LIFE CONCERNS

	2009-2010	2009-2010
	(N-119)	%
Losing Autonomy	104	87.39
Less able to engage in activities making life enjoyable	98	82.35
Loss of dignity	79	66.39
Losing control of bodily functions	53	44.54
Burden on family, friends/caregivers	29	24.37
Inadequate pain control or concern	35	29.41
Financial implications of treatment	4	3.36
totals	N/A	N/A

Of the 119 WDWDA population, 104 patients—(87%) named "losing autonomy" as their principal end of life concern; 98 patients—(82%) mentioned being "less able to engage in activities making life enjoyable;" more than half-79 patients—(66%) cited "loss of dignity;" and 53 patients—(45%) worried about "losing control of bodily functions."

On the issue of how their condition affected others, 29 patients—(24%) mentioned being a "burden on family friends/ caregivers."

"Inadequate pain control or concern about it" affected 35 patients—(29%).

Only 4 patients—(3%) worried about "financial implications of treatment." This should be cross-referenced to the fact that 2 percent of the 119 population had no insurance whatsoever.

B)-OREGON STATISTICS: Patients under the OREGON Act expressed like concerns as can be seen from the following comparison.

END OF LIFE CONCERNS: OREGON & WASHINGTON

	OREGON ACT	WASHINGTON ACT
	(N-525) %	**(N-119) %**
Losing Autonomy	90.48	87.39
Less able to engage in activities making life enjoyable	87.43	82.35
Loss of dignity	63.43	66.39
Losing control of bodily functions	56.00	44.54
Burden on family, friends/caregivers	35.05	24.37
Inadequate pain control or concern	21.14	29.41
Financial implications of treatment	2.48	3.36
totals	*N/A*	*N/A*

§6.04)-END OF LIFE CARE
A)-TABLE-4

END OF LIFE CARE

	2009-2010	2009-2010
	(N-119)	%
Hospice		
Enrolled	69	79.31
Not enrolled	15	17.24
Unknown	3	3.45
totals	87	100.00
NOTE: percentages computed from table totals.		
Insurance		
Private only	32	28.83
Medicare or Medicaid only	48	43.24
Combination of private and Medicare/Medicaid	18	16.22
None	2	1.80
Unknown	11	9.91
totals	111	100.00
NOTE: percentages computed from table totals.		

B)-HOSPICE CARE—79%: Of the 119 WDWDA population, a full 69 patients—(79%) were enrolled in hospice at the time they made the decision to end their lives by ingesting a lethal dose of medication. This statistic is surprising to those who hold to the belief that hospice is an effective alternative to the death with dignity acts.

Even more surprising is the fact that in 2007, the average (median) stay in an Oregon hospice program was only 18 days between admission and death. [*A Guidebook for Health Care Professionals*, sec. 4, cited in Appendix A.17 of this book]

1)-SUPREME COURT: In the 1997 Supreme Court case of Washington v. Glucksberg, the Coalition of Hospice Professionals filed an *Amici Curiae*—friend of the court—brief citing studies showing that: "[a]s death becomes more imminent, pain and suffering become progressively more difficult to treat") [Glucksberg at 748] To this observation regarding hospice care at the end of life, Justice Stevens in his concurring opinion stated: "An individual adequately informed of the care alternatives thus might make a rational choice for assisted suicide." [Id]

2)-OREGON ACT—86%: The Oregon experience was similar with 86% enrolled in hospice.

§6.05)-PROCESS
A)-TABLE-5

PROCESS

	2009-2010 (N-119)	2009-2010 %
Location of Patient's Death		
Home (patient, family or friend)	80	91.95
Long term care	2	2.30
Hospital	0	0.00
Other	3	3.45
Unknown	2	2.30
totals	87	100.00
NOTE: percentages computed from table totals.		
Lethal medication		
Secobarbital	110	92.44
Pentobarbital	8	6.72
Other	1	0.84
totals	119	100.00
Referred for mental evaluation	5	4.20
Patient informed family of decision	101	84.87

B)-PLACE OF DEATH: Of the 119 WDWDA population practically all, 80 patients—(92%), elected to die at either their own homes or those of a family member or close friend. Because the ingestion of the lethal dose of medication acted so quickly, there was less of a burden in choosing this most personal place to die. The Oregon Act saw 95% chose a like environment to die.

C)-LETHAL MEDICATION: The two lethal medications prescribed were Secobarbital for 110 patients—(92%), and Pentobarbital for 8 patients—(7%). Oregon patients also chose Secobarbital—61% and Pentabarbital—38%.

D)-PSYCHIATRIC EVALUATION: Only five patients—(4%) were referred for psychiatric evaluation in accordance with the Act's requirement for a "counseling referral":

> **Counseling referral.**
> If, in the opinion of the attending physician or the consulting physician, a patient may be suffering from a psychiatric or psychological disorder or **depression causing impaired judgment**, either physician shall refer the patient for counseling. Medication to end a patient's life in a humane and dignified manner shall not be prescribed until the person performing the counseling determines that the patient is not suffering from a psychiatric or psychological disorder or depression causing impaired judgment.
> [WDWDA RCW 70.245.060 (emphasis supplied)]

It should be noted that "impaired judgment," as used in the Washington Act, is not equivalent to the concept of lack of testamentary capacity.

Psychiatric evaluations under the Oregon Act amounted to 7%, almost twice the Washington referrals.

E)-DEPRESSION: Of course, depression can be expected to be present as patients face the reality of a terminal illness with less than six months to live, and experience the "end of life concerns" set forth in §6.03 above, However, it should be noted that it is not just "depression" that is at issue, but a "depression causing impaired judgment," a much higher standard.

F)-FAMILY NOTIFICATION: Most of the patients-101—(85%) elected to inform their families of their decision. The Act only requires the attending physician to "recommend" such disclosure; the patient is under no obligation to make that notification:

Notification of next of kin

The attending physician shall <u>recommend</u> that the patient notify the next of kin of his or her request for medication under this chapter. A patient who declines or is unable to notify next of kin shall not have his or her request denied for that reason.

[WDWDA RCW 70.245.080 (emphasis supplied)]

The Oregon patients chose to notify their families 81% of the time, similar to Washington's 85%.

§6.06)-TIMING OF EVENT
A)-TABLE-6

TIMING OF EVENT

	2009-2010	2009-2010
	(N-119)	**%**
Duration (weeks) of patient-physician relationship		
3-weeks – 24 weeks	57	51.35
25-weeks – 51 weeks	12	10.81
1 year or more	41	36.94
Unknown	1	0.90
totals	*111*	*100.00*
NOTE: percentages computed from table totals.		
2009 range: 3 weeks – 27 years		
2010 range: 3 weeks – 10 years		

	2009-2010	2009-2010
	(N-119)	%
Duration (days) between 1st oral request and death		
3-weeks – 24 weeks	102	91.89
25 weeks or more	8	7.21
Unknown	1	0.90
totals	*111*	*100.00*
NOTE: percentages computed from table totals.		
2009 range: 3 weeks – 43 weeks		
2010 range: 3 weeks – 54 weeks		
Time between ingestion and unconsciousness		
1 min – 10 min	61	70.11
11 min or more	9	10.34
Unknown	17	19.54
totals	*87*	*100.00*
NOTE: percentages computed from table totals.		
2009 range: 1 min – 20 min		
2010 range: 1 min – 30 min		
Time between ingestion and death		
1 min – 90 min	61	70.11
91 min or more	14	16.09
Unknown	12	13.79
totals	*87*	*100.00*
NOTE: percentages computed from table totals.		

B)-PATIENT-PHYSICIAN RELATIONSHIP: Half—(51%) of the patients had a relationship with their physicians of 3-weeks to 24 weeks. The conclusion that can be drawn from this statistic is that in many cases the physician involved in the prescription of the lethal dose of medication had no long-term relationship with the patient.

C)-TIME BETWEEN 1ST ORAL REQUEST AND DEATH:

The time between the first oral request for the prescription of the lethal dose of medication and death was 3-weeks to 24 weeks in 92% of the patients. The 3-week period, 21 days, is just about as fast as can be accomplished under the Act's 15 day waiting period.

D)-PHYSICIAN-ASSISTED DEATH—NOT SUICIDE: The

word "suicide" does not appear anywhere in the Washington Death with Dignity Act except in the following provision:

> **References to practices under this chapter**
>
> Nothing in this chapter authorizes a physician or any other person to end a patient's life by lethal injection, mercy killing, or active euthanasia. Actions taken in accordance with this chapter do not, for any purpose, constitute suicide, assisted suicide, mercy killing, or homicide, under the law. State reports shall not refer to practice under this chapter as "suicide" or "assisted suicide." …. state reports shall refer to practice under this chapter as obtaining and self-administering life-ending medication.
>
> [WDWDA RCW 70.245.180(1) (emphasis supplied)]

As a point of interest, early press releases from the Oregon Public Health Division referred to the program as "physician assisted suicide." [e.g., OHD Press Releases 2/17/99, 2/21/01, 3/5/03] In the March 15, 2011, OHD press release the practice was referred to as "physician-assisted death."

E)-BETWEEN INGESTION AND DEATH: The time between

ingestion and unconsciousness was between 1-10 minutes for 70% of the patients, with a 2009 range from 1-20 minutes, and a 2010 range from 1-30 minutes. The time between ingestion and death was between 1-90 minutes for 70% of the patients.

§6.07)-HEALTH-CARE PROVIDER PRESENT
A)-TABLE-7
HEALTH-CARE PROVIDER PRESENT

	2009-2010	2009-2010
	(N-119)	**%**
When medication was ingested		
Prescribing physician	5	5.75
Other provider (prescribing physician not present)	44	50.57
No provider	29	33.33
Unknown	9	10.34
totals	*87*	*100.00*

B)-PHYSICIAN PRESENT—6%: In only 5 cases—(6%) was the prescribing physician present when the lethal medication was ingested. In the Oregon experience, the prescribing physician was present when the lethal medication was ingested in 21% of the cases.

C)-OTHER PROVIDER PRESENT—51%: In 44 cases—(51%) a provider other than the prescribing physician was present when the lethal medication was ingested. Thus in 49 cases—(56%) of the cases either the physician or a provider was present at the time of death.

D)-NO PROVIDER PRESENT—33%: In 29 cases—(33%) no provider was present when the lethal medication was ingested. Of course this does not indicate which other individuals were present such as family members or friends.

E)-DISPOSAL OF UNUSED MEDICATIONS: As stated in the Washington Act: "Any medication dispensed under this chapter that was not self-administered shall be disposed of by lawful means," but no elaboration is provided. [WDWDA RCW 70.245.140]

§6.08)-COMPLICATIONS
A)-TABLE-8
COMPLICATIONS

	2009-2010	2009-2010
	(N-119)	%
No complication	75	86.21
Regurgitated	1	1.15
Seizures	0	0.00
Awakened after taking prescription	2	2.30
Unknown	9	10.34
totals	*87*	*100.00*

B)-NO COMPLICATIONS—86%: No complications were experienced by 75 patients—(86%). The Oregon figure is an almost identical 87%.

C)-REGURGITATION—1%: Regurgitation of the prescription was experienced by only 1 patient—(1%). The Oregon figure is much higher with 21 patients—(4%).

D)-AWAKENING—2%: Awakened after taking the prescription were 2 patients (2%). In Oregon the figure is 0.57%.

§6.09)-EMERGENCY MEDICAL SERVICES
A)-TABLE-9
EMERGENCY MEDICAL SERVICES

	2009-2010	2009-2010
	(N-119)	%
Not called after medication ingested	78	89.66
Called for intervention	0	0.00
Calls for other reasons	2	2.30
Unknown	7	8.05
totals	*87*	*100.00*

B)-NOT CALLED—90%: In the vast majority of cases-78 (90%) emergency medical services were not called following medication ingestion, and in no instance were they called for purposes of intervention.

C)-CALLED FOR OTHER REASONS: Those who called emergency medical services after ingesting a lethal dose of medication, but not for the reasons of intervention, were 2 in number (2%). This number included calls to pronounce death.

§6.10)-GENDER
A)-TABLE-10

GENDER

	2009-2010	2009-2010
	(N-119)	%
Male	62	52.10
Female	57	47.90
totals	119	100.00

The gender of the 119 WDWDA patients were almost evenly divided between men-62 patients—(52%), and women-57 patients—(48%).

§6.11)-AGE
A)-TABLE-11

AGE

	2009-2010	2009-2010
	(N-119)	%
18-34	0	0.00
35-44	0	0.00
45-54	10	8.40
55-64	23	19.33
65-74	40	33.61
75-84	28	23.53
85+	18	15.13
totals	119	100.00

As would be expected, over half-68 patients—(57%) of the 119 WDWDA patients were aged 65-84, with 18 patients—(15%) aged 85 and older. No patients were in the 18-44 age bracket.

The Oregon statistics were similar.

§6.12)-EDUCATION
A)-TABLE-12

EDUCATION

	2009-2010 (N-119)	2009-2010 %
Less than high school	7	6.86
High school graduate	32	31.37
Some college	20	19.61
Baccalaureate or higher	43	42.16
totals	102	100.00

As far as education was concerned, only 7 patients—(7%) did not graduate from high school, 32 patients—(31%) were high school graduates, 20 patients—(20%) had some college, and 43 patients—(42%) had baccalaureate degrees or higher.

The WDWDA level of education is considerably higher than that of both the national and Washington levels. The WDWDA percentage of those patients with a bachelor's degree or higher is 42% compared to a national average of 24.4% and a Washington average of 30.8%.

§6.13)-MARITAL STATUS
A)-TABLE-13

MARITAL STATUS

	2009-2010 (N-119)	2009-2010 %
Married	50	49.02
Widowed	28	27.45
Never Married	6	5.88
Divorced	18	17.65
totals	102	100.00

The marital status of the 102 reported WDWDA patients was as follows: 50 patient—(49%) were married at the time of their death, 28 patients—(27%) were widowed, 6 patients—(6%) were never married, and 18 patients—(18%) were divorced.

The Oregon statistics were similar: married—(47%), widowed—(22%), never married—(8%), and divorced—(23%).

§6.14)-RACE
A)-TABLE-14

RACE

	2009-2010	2009-2010
	(N-119)	%
Non-Hispanic White	98	96.08
Hispanic and/or Non-White	4	3.92
totals	102	100.00

National and Oregon information from U.S. Census [www.census.gov]

The race of the 102 reporting WDWDA patients was virtually all non-Hispanic white-98 patients—(96%). This number is higher than both the nation— 63.7% and Washington—72.5%, but of course it is only Washington that is relevant because the WDWDA only applies to Washington Residents.

Just as Washington had 96% white, Oregon had 98%.

§6.15)-PARTICIPATING PHYSICIANS

In 2010 in Washington, prescriptions were written for 87 patients, with 68 physicians and 40 pharmacists participating. [Washington Department of Health 2010 Report]

In Oregon, in the case of the first ten patients there were nine different attending physicians. [Oregon Press Release 8/18/98]

In Oregon in 2005, thirty-nine physicians wrote a total of 64 prescriptions for lethal doses of medication. [Oregon Press Release 3/9/06]

[page left blank]

CHAPTER-SEVEN

CRUZAN v. MISSOURI
SUPREME COURT 1990
497 U.S. 261 (1990)

CRUZAN WAS THE FIRST SUPREME COURT CASE DEALING WITH THE "RIGHT TO DIE." THE HOLDING OF THE COURT, AS IT RELATES TO THIS SUBJECT, WAS THAT PATIENTS HAVE THE RIGHT TO END THEIR LIVES BY REFUSING OR DISCONTINUING "DEATH PROLONGING PROCEDURES" AND "LIFE-SUSTAINING MEDICAL TREATMENT," SUCH AS "ARTIFICIALLY-DELIVERED FOOD AND WATER ESSENTIAL TO LIFE."

FACTS: The facts in Cruzan were not in dispute. As set forth by the Supreme Court via Chief Justice Rehnquist:

> Petitioner Nancy Beth Cruzan was rendered incompetent as a result of severe injuries sustained during an automobile accident. Copetitioners Lester and Joyce Cruzan, Nancy's parents and coguardians, sought a court order directing the **withdrawal of their daughter's artificial feeding and hydration** equipment after it became apparent that she had virtually no chance of recovering her cognitive faculties. ... In order to ease feeding and further the recovery, surgeons implanted a gastrostomy feeding and hydration tube in Cruzan.... She now lies in a Missouri state hospital in what is commonly referred to as a <u>persistent vegetative state</u>: generally, a condition in which a person exhibits motor reflexes but evinces no indications of significant cognitive function.... All agree that **such a removal would cause her death**.

[<u>Cruzan</u> at 265-68 (emphasis supplied)]

NOTES: This chapter/book does not contain legal advice, which can only be obtained by the reader's personal attorney. In order to let the Court speak for itself, commentary has been kept to a minimum.

SUBSTITUTED JUDGMENT and LIVING WILLS: In the absence of a living will, one of the principal questions in the Cruzan case was what degree of evidence of the patient's intent, expressed prior to her incapacity, would be sufficient to support her guardian's request. Since this issue is not relevant to the subject of the right to die, it has not been included in the analysis of this case for the purposes of this chapter.

RIGHT TO REFUSE TREATMENT: The Supreme Court of the State of Missouri in the Cruzan case, which opinion was the subject of the appeal to the United States Supreme Court, held that:

> [A] person in Nancy's condition had a fundamental right under the State and Federal Constitutions to refuse or direct the withdrawal of "death prolonging procedures."
>
> [Cruzan at 268, citing the Missouri state trial court]

COMMON LAW BATTERY: Prior, and in addition to, the codification of written laws in the United States, there was what was called "common law," also known as case law or precedent. This common law was developed by judges through decisions of courts. As it related to common law battery, the Supreme Court found:

> At common law, even the touching of one person by another without consent and without legal justification was a battery. [citation omitted] Before the turn of the century, this Court observed that "[n]o right is held more sacred, or is more carefully guarded, by the common law, than the right of every individual to the possession and control of his own person, free from all restraint or interference of others, unless by clear and unquestionable authority of law."
>
> [Cruzan at 269]

INFORMED CONSENT: An exception to common law battery for non-consensual touching, was when the individual gave permission through "informed consent":

> This notion of bodily integrity has been embodied in the requirement that informed consent is generally required for medical treatment. Justice Cardozo, while on the Court of Appeals of New York, aptly described this doctrine: "Every human being of adult years and sound mind has a right to determine what shall be done with his own body; and a surgeon who performs an operation without his patient's consent commits an assault, for which he is liable in damages." [citation omitted] The informed consent doctrine has become firmly entrenched in American tort law.
>
> [<u>Cruzan</u> at 269]

RIGHT TO REFUSE TREATMENT: Since a person has the right not to be touched except by informed consent, he/she has a right to refuse treatment:

> The logical corollary of the doctrine of informed consent is that the patient generally possesses the right not to consent, that is, to refuse treatment. Until about 15 years ago and the seminal decision in *In re Quinlan,* [1976] the number of <u>right-to-refuse-treatment</u> decisions were relatively few. …. More recently, however, with the <u>advance of medical technology capable of sustaining life</u> well past the point where natural forces would have brought certain death in earlier times, cases involving the **right to refuse life-sustaining treatment** have burgeoned….
>
> [<u>Cruzan</u> at 270 (emphasis supplied)]

ACTIVELY HASTENING DEATH: Death is a result of a patient's rejecting certain life sustaining treatments. Death is also a result of a patient's terminating the very same life sustaining treatment once it has been started. The question decided by a 1985

New Jersey case—In re Conroy, cited with approval by the Supreme Court, was stated as follows:

> The court also **rejected certain categorical distinctions** that had been drawn in prior refusal-of-treatment cases as lacking substance for decision purposes: the distinction between **actively hastening death by terminating treatment** and **passively allowing a person to die of a disease**; between **treating individuals as an initial matter** versus **withdrawing treatment afterwards**; between ordinary versus extraordinary treatment; and between treatment by artificial feeding versus other forms of life-sustaining medical procedures. [citation omitted]. As to the last item, the court acknowledged the "emotional significance" of food, but noted that feeding by implanted tubes is a "medical procedur[e] with inherent risks and possible side effects, instituted by skilled health-care providers to compensate for impaired physical functioning" which analytically was equivalent to artificial breathing using a respirator....

> [Cruzan at 273-74 (emphasis supplied)]

"RIGHT TO DIE": The Cruzan Court specifically acknowledged that they were faced with: "[T]he first case in which we have been squarely presented with the issue of whether the United States Constitution grants what is in common parlance referred to as a "right to die":

> The Fourteenth Amendment provides that no State shall "deprive any person of life, liberty, or property, without due process of law." The principle that a competent person has a constitutionally protected liberty interest in refusing unwanted medical treatment may be inferred from our prior decisions. [citation omitted]... [F]or purposes of this case, we assume that the United States Constitution would grant **a competent person a constitutionally protected right to refuse lifesaving hydration and nutrition**.

> [Cruzan at 278-79 (emphasis supplied)]

REJECTED TUBE TREATMENTS: In Justice O'Connor's concurring opinion in Cruzan, explicit references were made to nasogastric, gastrostomy and jejunostomy feeding tubes, as examples of treatments that a patient had a right to refuse:

> Whether or not the techniques used to pass food and water into the patient's alimentary tract are termed "medical treatment," it is clear they all involve some degree of intrusion and restraint. Feeding a patient by means of a nasogastric tube requires a physician to pass a long flexible tube through the patient's nose, throat and esophagus and into the stomach. Because of the discomfort such a tube causes, "[m]any patients need to be restrained forcibly and their hands put into large mittens to prevent them from removing the tube." [citation omitted] A gastrostomy tube (as was used to provide food and water to Nancy Cruzan, see *ante*, at 266) or jejunostomy tube must be surgically implanted into the stomach or small intestine. [citation omitted] Requiring a competent adult to endure such procedures against her will burdens the patient's liberty, dignity, and freedom to determine the course of her own treatment. Accordingly, the liberty guaranteed by the Due Process Clause must protect, if it protects anything, an individual's deeply personal decision to **reject medical treatment**, including the artificial delivery of food and water.
>
> [Cruzan at 288-89, O'Connor concurring (emphasis supplied)]

"SUICIDE" BY REJECTING MEDICAL TREATMENTS: In Justice Scalia's concurring opinion in Cruzan, he equates the refusal to utilize "measures necessary to preserve one's life" as "suicide":

> The various opinions in this case portray quite clearly the difficult, indeed agonizing, questions that are presented by the constantly increasing power of science to keep the human body alive for longer than any reasonable person

would want to inhabit it. ... American law has always accorded the State the power to prevent, by force if necessary, suicide including **suicide** <u>by refusing to take appropriate measures necessary to preserve one's life</u>; that the point at which life becomes "worthless," and the point at which the means necessary to preserve it become "extraordinary" or "inappropriate," are neither set forth in the Constitution nor known to the nine Justices of this Court any better than they are known to nine people picked at random from the Kansas City telephone directory....

[<u>Cruzan</u> at 292-93, Scalia concurring (emphasis supplied)]

"SUICIDE" BY "ACTION AND INACTION": In Justice Scalia's concurring opinion in <u>Cruzan</u>, he further discusses the dichotomy between suicide by action and inaction:

The second asserted distinction suggested by the recent cases canvassed by the Court concerning the right to refuse treatment, [citation omitted] relies on the **dichotomy between action and inaction**. Suicide, it is said, consists of an affirmative act to end one's life; refusing treatment is not an affirmative act "causing" death, but merely a passive acceptance of the natural process of dying. I readily acknowledge that the distinction between action and inaction has some bearing upon the legislative judgment of what ought to be prevented as suicide - though even there it would seem to me unreasonable to draw the line precisely between action and inaction, rather than between various forms of inaction. It would not make much sense to say that one may not kill oneself by walking into the sea, but may sit on the beach until submerged by the incoming tide; or that one may not intentionally lock oneself into a cold storage locker, but may refrain from coming indoors when the temperature drops below freezing. Even as a legislative matter, in other words, the intelligent line does not fall between action and inaction but between those forms of inaction that consist of abstaining from "ordinary" care and those that consist of abstaining from "excessive" or "heroic" measures. Unlike action *vs.* inaction, that is not a line to be discerned by logic or legal analysis, and we should not pretend that it is. ...But to return to the principal point for present purposes: the irrelevance of the action-inaction distinction. **Starving oneself to death** is no different from **putting a gun to one's temple** as far as the common-law definition of suicide is concerned; the cause of death in both cases is the suicide's conscious decision to "pu[t] an end to his own existence." [citation omitted] Of course the common law rejected the action-inaction distinction in other contexts involving the taking of human life as well.

[Cruzan at 296-97, Scalia concurring (emphasis supplied)]

SUICIDE BY SLASHING WRITS AND OVERDOSING: In

Justice Scalia's concurring opinion in Cruzan, he further discusses a patient's attempt's to commit suicide by slashing his wrists and taking an overdose of barbiturates, and a hospital's life saving efforts and responsibilities:

It is not even reasonable, much less required by the Constitution, to maintain that although the State has the right to prevent a person from **slashing his wrists**, it does not have the power to apply physical force to prevent him from doing so, nor the power, should he succeed, to apply, coercively if necessary, medical measures to stop the flow of blood. The state-run hospital, I am certain, is not liable under [citation omitted] for violation of constitutional rights, nor the private hospital liable under general tort law, if, in a State where suicide is unlawful, it pumps out the stomach of a person who has **intentionally taken an overdose of barbiturates**, despite that person's wishes to the contrary.

[Cruzan at 298-99, Scalia concurring (emphasis supplied)]

MERGER OF BODY AND MACHINE: In Justice Stevens dissenting opinion, he poetically finds a "merger of body and machine that some might reasonably regard as an insult to life rather than as its continuation":

> Medical advances have altered the physiological conditions of death in ways that may be alarming: highly invasive treatment may perpetuate human existence through a **merger of body and machine** that some might reasonably regard as **an insult to life, rather than as its continuation.** But those same advances, and the reorganization of medical care accompanying the new science and technology, have also transformed the political and social conditions of death: people are less likely to die at home, and more likely to die in relatively public places, such as hospitals or nursing homes. Ultimate questions that might once have been dealt with in intimacy by a family and its physician have now become the concern of institutions. When the institution is a state hospital, as it is in this case, the government itself becomes involved. Dying nonetheless remains a part of "the life which characteristically has its place in the home" [citation omitted].
>
> [Cruzan at 339-40, Stevens dissenting (emphasis supplied)]

APPRECIATION OF MORTALITY: In equally poetic terms, Justice Stevens in his dissenting opinion, speaks of an "appreciation of mortality":

> The more precise constitutional significance of death is difficult to describe; not much may be said with confidence about death unless it is said from faith, and that alone is reason enough to protect the freedom to conform choices about death to individual conscience. We may also, however, justly assume that death is not life's simple opposite, or its necessary terminus, but rather its completion. Our ethical tradition has long regarded an appreciation of mortality as essential to

understanding life's significance. It may, in fact, be impossible to live for anything without being prepared to die for something. Certainly there was no disdain for life in Nathan Hale's most famous declaration or in Patrick Henry's; their words instead bespeak a passion for life that forever preserves their own lives in the memories of their countrymen. From such "honored dead we take increased devotion to that cause for which they gave the last *full measure of devotion.*"

[<u>Cruzan</u> at 343-44, Stevens dissenting (emphasis supplied)]

REMEMBERANCE OF LIFE: A patient has an interest in how he/she will be remembered by loved ones:

> …Nancy Cruzan's interest in life, no less than that of any other person, includes an <u>interest in how she will be thought of after her death</u> by those whose opinions mattered to her. There can be no doubt that her life made her dear to her family, and to others. <u>How she dies will affect how that life is remembered</u>.

[<u>Cruzan</u> at 344, Stevens dissenting (emphasis supplied)]

DEFINITION OF LIFE: Definitions of human life can be based on theological or philosophical conjecture—not permitted under the Constitution; or by a sectarian definition—a permitted basis:

> In short, there is no reasonable ground for believing that Nancy Beth Cruzan has any *personal* interest in the perpetuation of what the State has decided is her life. As I have already suggested, it would be possible to hypothesize such an interest on the basis of **theological or philosophical conjecture**. But even to posit such a basis for the State's action is to condemn it. It is not within the province of secular government to circumscribe the liberties of the people by regulations designed wholly for the purpose of establishing a **sectarian definition of life**. [citation omitted]

[<u>Cruzan</u> at 350, Stevens dissenting (emphasis supplied)]

INTERESTS IN DEATH: While there are obvious interests in life, there are also interests in a timely death:

> Insofar as Nancy Cruzan has an **interest in being remembered** for how she lived rather than how she died, the damage done to those memories by the prolongation of her death is irreversible. Insofar as Nancy Cruzan has an **interest in the cessation of any pain**, the continuation of her pain is irreversible. Insofar as Nancy Cruzan has an **interest in a closure to her life** consistent with her own beliefs rather than those of the Missouri legislature, the State's imposition of its contrary view is irreversible. To deny the importance of these consequences is in effect to deny that Nancy Cruzan has interests at all, and thereby to deny her personhood in the name of preserving the sanctity of her life.
>
> [Cruzan at 353, Stevens dissenting (emphasis supplied)]

CONCLUSION

Even though the 1990 Supreme Court decision in Cruzan v. Missouri predated the Oregon Death with Dignity Act of 1994/1997, the opinion is relevant in as much as it was the first case to deal with the concept of a "right to die," by a patient's voluntarily refusing life sustaining food and water.

The case was so important that in addition to the Court's decision written by Chief Justice Rehnquist (joined in by Justices White, O'connor, Scalia and Kennedy), concurring opinions by Justices O'Connor and Scalia, and a dissenting opinion by Justice Brennan (joined in by Justices Marshall and Blackmun) and another dissenting opinion by Justice Stevens.

All these opinions discussed the central issue of what constitutes the right to refuse life-sustaining medical treatments, suicide, and how far an individual can go in determine his/her manner and time of death.

CHAPTER-EIGHT
WASHINGTON v. GLUCKSBERG
SUPREME COURT 1997
521 U.S. 702

GLUCKSBERG UPHELD A WASHINGTON STATE BAN AGAINST PHYSICIAN-ASSISTED SUICIDE. BUT MORE IMPORTANTLY, THE COURT ACKNOWLEDGED THE EXISTENCE OF THE OREGON DEATH WITH DIGNITY ACT, AND INDICATED THAT IT WAS WITHIN THE PURVIEW OF EACH STATE TO EITHER CONTINUE SUCH A BAN OR ADOPT LEGISLATION PERMITTING THE PRACTICE.

PRIMARY TENSION: The primary tension in the area of physician-assisted suicide is between: a)-employing medication to alleviate pain even though it "**hastens death**," (a legally accepted medical practice throughout the United States); and, b)-prescribing a lethal dose of medication to "**cause death**," (a practice traditionally thought of as homicide). The 1997 Supreme Court decision in <u>Washington v. Glucksberg</u>, deals with this tension, and upholds the above distinction.

DEATH WITH DIGNITY ACTS: It was not until the adoption of Death with Dignity Acts in the State of Oregon in 1994, and the State of Washington in 2008, that prescribing "medication to end [a qualified patient's] life in a humane and dignified manner," was made legal for residents of these two states. As of the end of 2011, Oregon and Washington were the only states with such legislation.

WASHINGTON'S ASSISTED SUICIDE LAW: In a nutshell, <u>Washington v. Glucksberg</u>, upheld the State of Washington's statute prohibiting "caus[ing] or "aid[ing] a suicide, and making

NOTES: This chapter/book does not contain legal advice, which can only be obtained by the reader's personal attorney. In order to let the Court speak for itself, commentary has been kept to a minimum.

such assistance a felony. This Washington statute was in effect when the Supreme Court decided Glucksberg in 1997, and before this state's adoption of its Death with Dignity Act in 2008. The relevancy of the Glucksberg decision, as of the end of 2011, is that it is the law throughout the United States except for Oregon and Washington, and possibly Montana. The Supreme Court leaves it up to the legislature of each state to define physician-assisted suicide—an illegal act, and physician-assisted death under Death with Dignity Acts—a legal practice.

THE ROAD TO THE SUPREME COURT: So controversial was the question of physician-assisted suicide that the Glucksberg case followed a torturous road through the federal judiciary, as well as in the Supreme Court.

The first court—the federal District Court, held Washington's statute prohibiting physician-assisted suicide to be unconstitutional.

A three judge panel of the Court of Appeals for the Ninth Circuit, which next heard the case, reversed the District Court and upheld the state's ban against physician-assisted suicide.

Next, the same Ninth Circuit hearing the case en banc (all judges in the circuit), reversed the first three judge panel's decision and affirmed the original opinion by the District Court striking down the ban.

The Supreme Court then heard the case and reversed the Ninth Circuit's en banc opinion, upholding the Washington statute.

To add to this complexity, not to say confusion, the Supreme Court issued five separate opinions. First was the main opinion written by Chief Justice Rehnquist, joined in by Justices O'Connor, Scalia, Kennedy and Thomas. Second was a concurring opinion by Justice O'Connor joined in part by Justices Ginsburg and Breyer. And, third through five were separate concurring opinions by Justices Stevens, Ginsburg and Breyer.

PLAINTIFFS: The original plaintiffs in this case were: (a) Dr. Glucksberg and several of his colleagues who "occasionally treat terminally ill, suffering patients, and stated that they would assist these patients in ending their lives if not for Washington's assisted-suicide ban," and (b) three of their patients. [<u>Glucksberg</u> at 707] The original defendant was the State of Washington.

The Ninth Circuit Court of Appeals, and the Glucksberg plaintiffs, succinctly stated the issues as: "Is there a right to die," and a right to "control of one's final days," and described the asserted liberty as "the right to choose a humane, dignified death," and "the liberty to shape death." [<u>Glucksberg</u> at 722]

WASHINGTON'S ASSISTED SUICIDE LAW: Washington's anti-assisted suicide law, as it appeared in that state's criminal law in 1997, contained a felony provision, stated as follows:

> "A person is guilty of promoting a suicide attempt when he knowingly causes or aids another person to attempt suicide." [citation omitted] "Promoting a suicide attempt" is a felony, punishable by up to five years' imprisonment and up to a $10,000 fine.
>
> [<u>Glucksberg</u> at 707]

WASHINGTON'S WITHHOLDING TREATMENT LAW:
Now consider another Washington statute dealing with life-sustaining treatments:

> "...withholding or withdrawal of life-sustaining treatment" at a patient's direction "shall not, for any purpose, constitute a suicide."
>
> [<u>Glucksberg</u> at 707]

MURDER: It should be here noted that referencing the first of the above set forth statutes "promoting of a suicide attempt," if successful, would make the promoter, whether a physician or not, an accomplice to "murder." On this point, the Supreme Court cited with approval an historical authority on Connecticut law which stated: "[i]f one counsels another to commit suicide, and the other by reason of the advice kills himself, the advisor is guilty of murder as principal." A similar quotation held: "Now if the murder of one's self is felony, the accessory is equally guilty as if he had aided and abetted in the murder." [Glucksberg at 714] As to the nature of the conduct that will constitute "counsel[ing]" and being an "accessory" consider an historic New York State statute that included within this category: "furnish[ing] another person with any deadly weapon or poisonous drug, knowing that such person intends to use such weapon or drug in taking his own life." [Glucksberg at 715]

SHORTENING LIFE: Another point that is central to the issue of timing, holds that shortening an individual's life is murder, and is equally punishable whether the life is shortened by only a few minutes or when the victim is in the prime of life. To illustrate and emphasis this point the Supreme Court cited an historical case that held: "[A] prisoner who persuaded another to commit suicide could be tried for murder, even though <u>victim was scheduled shortly to be executed</u>." [Glucksberg at 715 (emphasis supplied)] The reason why this point is so important is that there are some medical prescripttions and practices that will have the side effect of shortening a patient's life.

The final Court of Appeals decision, before being reversed by the Supreme Court, stated that its opinion in favor of physician-assisted suicide, was based in part on "'historical and current societal attitudes' toward suicide and assisted suicide." [Glucksberg at 709]

AMICUS CURIAE BRIEFS: Getting into the fray at all levels of the case were additional entities. <u>Compassion in Dying</u> "a nonprofit organization that counsels people considering physician-assisted suicide," [Glucksberg at 708] joined the suit at the District Court level seeking a declaration that the statute was unconstitutional.

The <u>United States Department of Justice</u> filed an *amicus curiae* brief in support of the validity of the statute.

PROTECTION OF HUMAN LIFE: At the beginning of the Supreme Court's opinion in <u>Glucksberg</u>, the basic statement was made concerning the "protection and preservation of all human life," followed by a recitation of the "700 years of Anglo-American...tradition" disapproving of both suicide and assisting therein:

> In almost every State—indeed, in almost every western democracy—it is a crime to assist a suicide. The States' assisted-suicide bans are not innovations. Rather, they are longstanding expressions of the States' commitment to the <u>protection and preservation of all human life [citing Cruzan]</u>.
>
> . . . . .
>
> Indeed, opposition to and condemnation of suicide—and, therefore, of assisting suicide—are consistent and enduring themes of our philosophical, legal, and cultural heritages. [citation omitted] More specifically, for over <u>700 years, the Anglo-American common-law tradition</u> has punished or otherwise disapproved of both suicide and assisting suicide.
>
> [<u>Glucksberg</u> at 710-11 (emphasis supplied)]

WITHDRAWAL OF REFUSAL OF LIFE SUSTAINING MEDICAL TREATMENT: In some instances medical advances in life-sustaining machines can now prolong a patient's terminal illness at the cost of ever increasing pain and suffering, to both the patient and to those who are the patient's beloved. In other instances removal from such devices will, without medical doubt, certainly bring about the patient's death, but at the cost of ever increasing, unbearable and excruciating anguish. What to do? Administer higher and higher pain medication with the foreseeable result of shortening the life of the patient, but with the patient's continuing residual pain, or administer the ultimate pain relieving medication in the form of physician-assisted suicide. The Supreme Court was not unmindful of this dilemma:

> Because of advances in medicine and technology, Americans today are increasingly likely to die in institutions, from chronic illnesses. [citation omitted] Public concern and democratic action are therefore sharply focused on how best to protect dignity and independence at the end of life, with the result that there have been many significant changes in state laws and in the attitudes these laws reflect. Many States, for example, now permit "living wills," surrogate health-care decision making, and the **withdrawal or refusal of life-sustaining medical treatment**.
>
> [Glucksberg at 716 (emphasis supplied)]

The Court did acknowledge the patient's absolute right to refuse medical treatment: "We have also assumed, and strongly suggested, that the Due Process Clause protects the traditional right to refuse unwanted life saving medical treatment." "We assumed that the Constitution granted competent persons a 'constitutionally protected right to refuse lifesaving hydration and nutrition.'" [Glucksberg at 720 and 723, citing Cruzan, 497 U.S., at 278-279] Within the context of "shortening" a patient's life by, on the one hand removal of life-support mechanisms, and on the other hand by physician-assisted suicide, the Court of Appeals in their first opinion found the two to be similar enough to strike down the Washington State's ban on assisted suicide:

> [Plaintiffs] contend that in *Cruzan* we "acknowledged that competent, dying persons have the **right to direct the removal of life-sustaining medical treatment** and thus **hasten death**," [citation omitted] and that "the constitutional principle behind recognizing the patient's liberty to direct the withdrawal of artificial life support applies at least as strongly to the choice to **hasten impending death** by **consuming lethal medication**,"

[citation omitted] Similarly, the Court of Appeals concluded that "Cruzan, by recognizing a liberty interest that includes the refusal of artificial provision of life-sustaining food and water, necessarily recognize[d] a liberty interest in hastening one's own death."

[<u>Glucksberg</u> at 725 (emphasis supplied) (bracket in original)]

The Supreme Court did not agree with the plaintiffs' claim of controlling comparison:

> The right assumed in <u>Cruzan</u>, however, was not simply deduced from abstract concepts of personal autonomy. Given the common-law rule that forced medication was a battery, and the long legal tradition protecting the decision to refuse unwanted medical treatment, our assumption was entirely consistent with this Nation's history and constitutional traditions. <u>The decision to commit suicide with the assistance of another may be just as personal and profound as the decision to refuse unwanted medical treatment, but it has never enjoyed similar legal protection.</u> Indeed, the two acts are widely and reasonably regarded as quite distinct.

[<u>Glucksberg</u> at 725 (emphasis supplied)]

PALLIATIVE CASE HASTENING DEATH: In the concurring opinion of Justice O'Connor the issue of the legal hastening of death through medication is squarely dealt with:

> The parties and *amici* agree that in these States a patient who is suffering from a terminal illness and who is experiencing great pain has no legal barriers to obtaining <u>medication</u>, from qualified physicians, <u>to alleviate that suffering, even to the point of causing unconsciousness and</u> **hastening death**. [citation omitted]
>
> . . . . .
>
> There is no dispute that dying patients in Washington and New York can obtain **palliative care**, even when doing so would **hasten their deaths**.

[<u>Glucksberg</u> at 736-738 J. O'Connor
concurring opinion (emphasis supplied)]

OREGON DEATH WITH DIGNITY ACT: While the Supreme Court continued to examine the "700 years of Anglo-American...tradition" disapproving assisted-suicide, it did recognize an exception in Oregon with that State's passing of its Death with Dignity Act:

> On the other hand, in 1994, voters in Oregon enacted, also through ballot initiative, that State's "Death With Dignity Act," which legalized physician-assisted suicide for competent, terminally ill adults.
>
> [Glucksberg at 717]

SLIPPERY-SLOPE ARGUMENT: The Supreme Court also recognized the so-called "slippery-slope argument," which fears that today's voluntary physician-assisted suicide will result in tomorrow's involuntary and semi-involuntary "suicides" of the weak and vulnerable: Citing New York State's Task Force on Life and the Law, the Court found:

> After studying physician-assisted suicide, however, the Task Force unanimously concluded that "[l]egalizing assisted suicide and euthanasia would pose profound risks to many individuals who are ill and vulnerable. . . . [T]he potential dangers of this dramatic change in public policy would outweigh any benefit that might be achieved."
>
> [Glucksberg at 719 (bracket in original)]

and:

> [T]he State has an interest in protecting vulnerable groups—including the poor, the elderly, and disabled persons—from abuse, neglect, and mistakes. The Court of Appeals dismissed the State's concern that disadvantaged persons might be pressured into physician-assisted suicide as "ludicrous on its face." [citation omitted] We have recognized, however, the real risk of **subtle coercion** and **undue influence** in end-of-life situations. [citing Cruzan] Similarly, the New York Task

Force warned that "[l]egalizing physician-assisted suicide would pose profound risks to many individuals who are **ill and vulnerable**. . . . The risk of harm is greatest for the many individuals in our society whose autonomy and well-being are already compromised by poverty, lack of access to good medical care, advanced age, or membership in a stigmatized social group.

. . . . .

Finally, the State may fear that permitting assisted suicide will start it down the path to voluntary and perhaps even involuntary euthanasia.

[Glucksberg at 731-732]

Justice Souter also raised the spectra of the "slippery slope":

Whether acting from compassion or under some other influence, a physician who would provide a drug for a patient to administer might well go the further step of administering the drug himself; so, the barrier between assisted suicide and euthanasia could become porous, and the line between voluntary and **involuntary euthanasia** as well. The case for the **slippery slope** is fairly made out here, not because recognizing one due process right would leave a court with no principled basis to avoid recognizing another, but because there is a plausible case that the right claimed would not be readily containable by reference to facts about the mind that are matters of difficult judgment, or by gatekeepers who are subject to temptation, noble or not.

[Glucksberg at 784-785, Justice Souter (emphasis supplied)]

DEPRESSION: One of the most difficult provisions in the Oregon Death with Dignity Act is the requirement for "counseling" if the patient is suffering from depression:

"**Counseling**" means one or more consultations as necessary between a state licensed psychiatrist or psychologist and a patient for the purpose of determining that the patient is capable and not suffering from a

> psychiatric or **psychological disorder** or **depression** causing impaired judgment.
>
> [ODWDA 127.800 §1.01(5) (emphasis supplied)]

But for the specific provision concerning depression in the Oregon statute, it could almost go without saying that a terminally ill patient suffering tremendous pain and suffering at the end of life is also depressed. But the provision is in the statute, and the Supreme Court in its opinion dealt with this issue at considerable length:

> Those who attempt suicide—terminally ill or not—often suffer from **depression** or **other mental disorders**. See New York Task Force … (more than 95% of those who commit suicide had a major psychiatric illness at the time of death; among the terminally ill, uncontrolled pain is a "risk factor" because it contributes to depression); [citation omitted] ("[I]ntolerable physical symptoms are not the reason most patients request physician-assisted suicide or euthanasia"). Research indicates, however, that many people who request physician-assisted suicide withdraw that request if their depression and pain are treated. [citation omitted] (suicidal, terminally ill patients "usually respond well to treatment for depressive illness and pain medication and are then grateful to be alive"); [citation omitted] The New York Task Force, however, expressed its concern that, because depression is difficult to diagnose, physicians and medical professionals often fail to respond adequately to seriously ill patients' needs. [citation omitted] Thus, legal physician-assisted suicide could make it more difficult for the State to protect depressed or mentally ill persons, or those who are suffering from untreated pain, from suicidal impulses.
>
> [Glucksberg at 730-731 (emphasis supplied)]

The Court also cited the Code of Ethics of the American Medical Association which states: "[p]hysician-assisted suicide is fundamentally incompatible with the physician's role as healer."

[Glucksberg at 731 (bracket in original)]

DEATH PENALTY: Justice Stevens, in his concurring opinion, for the first time in the case brings up the observation that the State of Washington has the death penalty:

> A State, like Washington, that has authorized the **death penalty**, and thereby has concluded that the sanctity of human life does not require that it always be preserved, must acknowledge that **there are situations in which an interest in hastening death is legitimate**. Indeed, not only is that interest sometimes legitimate, I am also convinced that there are times when it is entitled to constitutional protection.
>
> [Glucksberg at 741-742, Justice Stevens (emphasis supplied)]

DIGNIFIED MEMORIES: Justice Stevens, in his concurring opinion, broached a unique consideration concerning dying with dignity for the memories of the patient's beloved, as well as the reality of living with "intolerable pain":

> I insist that the source of Nancy Cruzan's right to refuse treatment was not just a common-law rule. Rather, this right is an aspect of a far broader and more basic concept of freedom that is even older than the common law. This freedom embraces not merely a person's right to refuse a particular kind of unwanted treatment, but also her interest in **dignity**, and in determining the character of the memories that will survive long after her death.
>
> . . . . .
>
> Avoiding **intolerable pain** and the indignity of living one's final days incapacitated and in agony is certainly "[a]t the heart of [the] liberty. . . to define one's own concept of existence, of meaning, of the universe, and of the mystery of human life." [citation omitted]
>
> . . . . .
>
> Although there is no absolute right to physician-assisted suicide, *Cruzan* makes it clear that some individuals who no longer have the option of deciding whether to live or to die because they are already on the threshold of death

have a constitutionally protected interest that may outweigh the State's interest in preserving life at all costs. The liberty interest at stake in a case like this differs from, and is stronger than, both the common-law right to refuse medical treatment and the unbridled interest in deciding whether to live or die. It is an interest in deciding how, rather than whether, a critical threshold shall be crossed.

[Glucksberg at 743-745, Justice Stevens (emphasis supplied)]

TERMINAL SEDATION: Justice Stevens, in his concurring opinion, also makes specific mention of "medication that may hasten death" and "terminal sedation":

That interest [in the sanctity of life] not only justifies—it commands—maximum protection of every individual's interest in remaining alive, which in turn commands the same protection for decisions about whether to commence or to terminate life-support systems or to administer **pain medication that may hasten death**.

. . . . .

There are those who will want to continue aggressive treatment; those who would prefer **terminal sedation**; and those who will seek withdrawal from life-support systems and death by gradual **starvation** and **dehydration**. Although as a general matter the State's interest in the contributions each person may make to society outweighs the person's interest in ending her life, this interest does not have the same force for a **terminally ill patient faced not with the choice of whether to live, only of how to die**.

. . . . .

[E]nsuring the availability of adequate pain treatment is of utmost importance; **palliative care**, however, cannot alleviate all pain and suffering.

. . . . .

see also Brief for Coalition of **Hospice** Professionals as *Amici Curiae* 8 (citing studies showing that "[a]s death becomes more imminent, pain and suffering become progressively more difficult to treat"). An individual adequately informed of the care alternatives thus might make a rational choice for assisted suicide.

[<u>Glucksberg</u> at 746-748, Justice Stevens (emphasis supplied)]

INTENT: The argument of "double effect," or this author's preference for the terminology of "primary intention" and "secondary consequence," speaks to an action that has two results—one intentional and the other consequential. Therefore, the question: what is the primary intention of a physician that administers terminal medication to a dying patient requesting such treatment? Justice Stevens in his concurring opinion addresses just that issue:

> There may be little distinction between the intent of a terminally ill patient who decides to remove her life support and one who seeks the assistance of a doctor in ending her life; in both situations, the patient is seeking to hasten a certain, impending death. The **doctor's intent** might also be the same in **prescribing lethal medication** as it is in **terminating life support**. A doctor who fails to administer medical treatment to one who is dying from a disease could be doing so with an intent to harm or kill that patient. Conversely, **a doctor who prescribes lethal medication does not necessarily intend the patient's death—rather that doctor may seek simply to ease the patient's suffering** and to comply with her wishes. The illusory character of any differences in intent or causation is confirmed by the fact that the American Medical Association unequivocally endorses the practice of **terminal sedation**—the administration of sufficient dosages of pain-killing medication to terminally ill patients to protect them from excruciating pain even when it is clear that the **time of death will be advanced**. The purpose of terminal sedation is to ease the suffering of the patient and comply with her wishes, and the actual

cause of death is the administration of heavy doses of lethal sedatives.

[Glucksberg at 750-751, Justice Stevens (emphasis supplied)]

In like manner to Justice Stevens concurring opinion set forth above, Justice Souter also wrote a concurring opinion discussing "primary intent":

> Washington, like other States, authorizes physicians to withdraw life-sustaining medical treatment and artificially delivered food and water from patients who request it, even though such actions will **hasten death**. [citation omitted] The State permits physicians to alleviate anxiety and discomfort when withdrawing artificial life-supporting devices by administering medication that will **hasten death even further**. And it generally permits physicians to administer medication to patients in terminal conditions when the **primary intent** is to alleviate pain, even when the medication is so powerful as to hasten death and the patient chooses to receive it with that understanding.
>
> [Glucksberg at 780, Justice Souter (emphasis supplied)]

Justice Breyer in his concurring opinion states that:

> [T]he laws of New York and of Washington do not prohibit doctors from providing patients with **drugs sufficient to control pain** despite the **risk that those drugs themselves will kill**.
>
> . . . . .
>
> Medical technology, we are repeatedly told, makes the administration of pain-relieving drugs sufficient, except for a very few individuals for whom the ineffectiveness of pain control medicines can mean not pain, but the need for sedation
>
> [Glucksberg at 791, Justice Breyer (emphasis supplied)]

CONCLUSION

The 1997 Supreme Court decision in Washington v. Glucksberg can, on the one hand, be narrowly construed as a case simply upholding the right of a state to include a ban on assisted suicide in its criminal statutes. On the other hand, besides acknowledging the existence of the Oregon Death with Dignity Act, the Court laid the groundwork for validating future states' Death with Dignity Acts. In other words, it is the right of every state to either: place a ban on assisted-suicide, or adopt statutes permitting physician-assisted death, such as the Oregon Act.

Nine years after the 1997 <u>Glucksberg</u> decision, the Supreme Court had another opportunity to address the issues of physician-assisted death. This 2006 case is captioned <u>Gonzales v. Oregon</u>, and is the subject of the next chapter of this book.

[page left blank]

CHAPTER-NINE
GONZALES v. OREGON
SUPREME COURT 2006
546 U.S. 243

ATTORNEY GENERAL JOHN ASHCROFT OVER-STEPPED HIS AUTHORITY WHEN HE, IN EFFECT, TRIED TO OVERTURN THE OREGON DEATH WITH DIGNITY ACT THROUGH THE DEVICE OF ISSUING AN "INTERPRETIVE RULE." THIS RULE HELD THAT THE PRESCRIPTION OF A LETHAL DOSE OF MEDICATION TO END A PATIENT'S LIFE WAS AGAINST THE FEDERAL CONTROLLED SUBSTANCES ACT.

VOTERS REFERENDUMS: In 1994, a voters' referendum in the State of Oregon was decided in favor of adopting the Oregon Death with Dignity Act ("ODWDA" or "the Oregon Act"). This statute, for the first time in the history of the United States, permitted physician-assisted suicide, or as the proponents of such legislation prefer to term it "physician-assisted death." The vote was 51% for, and 49% against. In 1997 the voters of Oregon once again went to the polls and reaffirmed the Act with a vote of 60% for, and 40% against.

As would be expected, this Oregon Act was passed over the vigorous opposition of both traditional medical organizations and the pro-life movement.

ASHCROFT'S "INTERPRETIVE RULE": What the opposetion could not accomplish at the ballot boxes, Attorney General John Ashcroft attempted to do by a 2001 "Interpretive Rule" which determined that the prescription of a lethal dose of medication was in violation of the federal Controlled Substance Act.

NOTES: This chapter/book does not contain legal advice, which can only be obtained by the reader's personal attorney. In order to let the Court speak for itself, commentary has been kept to a minimum.

As framed by the Supreme Court:

> The drugs Oregon physicians prescribe under ODWDA are regulated under a federal statute, the **Controlled Substances Act (CSA)** [citation omitted] [This Act] allows these particular drugs to be available only by a written prescription from a registered physiccian. In the ordinary course the same drugs are prescribed in smaller doses for pain alleviation.
>
> A November 9, 2001, Interpretive Rule issued by the Attorney General [John Ashcroft] addresses the implementation and enforcement of the CSA with respect to ODWDA. It determines that **using controlled substances to assist suicide is not a legitimate medical practice** and that dispensing or prescribing them for this purpose is unlawful under the CSA. The Interpretive Rule's validity under the CSA is the issue before us.
>
> [Gonzales at 249 (emphasis supplied)]

OBLIQUE ATTACK AGAINST THE ODWDA: The Court observed from the outset that Ashcroft's "Interpretive Rule" was nothing more than an oblique attack against the Oregon Act:

> The importance of the issue of physician-assisted suicide, which has been the subject of an "earnest and profound debate" across the country, *Glucksberg,* 521 U.S., at 735, makes the oblique form of the claimed delegation all the more suspect.
>
> [Gonzales at 267 (emphasis supplied)]

THE OREGON DEATH WITH DIGNITY ACT: The Court then set forth with great detail the relevant components of the Oregon Death with Dignity Act:

> Oregon voters enacted ODWDA in 1994. For Oregon residents to be eligible to request a prescription under ODWDA, they must receive a diagnosis from their attending physician that they have an incurable and irreversible disease that, within reasonable medical judgment, will cause death within six months. [citation to

ODWDA] Attending physicians must also determine whether a patient has made a <u>voluntary request</u>, ensure a patient's <u>choice is informed</u>, and refer patients to counseling if they might be suffering from a psychological disorder or <u>depression causing impaired judgment</u>. [citation to ODWDA] A second <u>"consulting"</u> <u>physician</u> must examine the patient and the medical record and confirm the attending physician's conclusions. [citation to ODWDA] <u>Oregon physicians</u> may dispense or issue a prescription for the requested drug, but <u>may not administer it</u>. [citation to ODWDA] The reviewing physicians must keep <u>detailed medical records</u> of the process leading to the final prescription, [citation to ODWDA] records that Oregon's Department of Human Services reviews [citation to ODWDA] Physicians who dispense medication pursuant to ODWDA must also be <u>registered</u> with both the State's Board of Medical Examiners and the <u>federal Drug Enforcement Administration (DEA)</u>. [citation to ODWDA] ... In 2004, 37 patients ended their lives by ingesting a lethal dose of medication prescribed under ODWDA.

[<u>Gonzales</u> at 251-52 (emphasis supplied)]

THE POLITICAL FACTOR: To establish that <u>Gonzales</u> was a purely political matter, the Court took considerable pains to set forth the history leading up to Ashcroft's Interpretive Rule:

> <u>In 1997, Members of Congress</u> concerned about ODWDA invited the DEA to prosecute or revoke the CSA registration of Oregon physicians who assist suicide. They <u>contended that hastening a patient's death</u> <u>is not legitimate medical practice, so prescribing</u> <u>controlled substances for that purpose violates the CSA</u>. Letter from Sen. Orrin Hatch and Rep. Henry Hyde ... (July 25, 1997), ... The letter received an initial, favorable response from the director of the DEA [citation omitted], but Attorney General Reno considered the

matter and concluded that the DEA could not take the proposed action....

In 2001, John Ashcroft was appointed Attorney General. ... Mr. Ashcroft had supported efforts to curtail assisted suicide while serving as a Senator....

[Gonzales at 252-53 (emphasis supplied)]

Ashcroft left no doubt that his Interpretive Rule was directed against the prescribing physicians:

"[A]ssisting suicide is not a 'legitimate medical purpose' within the meaning of [the Controlled Substance Act] (2001), and that prescribing, dispensing, or administering federally controlled substances to assist suicide violates the Controlled Substances Act. Such conduct by a physician registered to dispense controlled substances may 'render his registration . . . inconsistent with the public interest' and therefore subject to possible suspension or revocation. [citation omitted] The Attorney General's conclusion applies regardless of whether state law authorizes or permits such conduct by practitioners or others and regardless of the condition of the person whose suicide is assisted."

[Gonzales at 254 (emphasis supplied)]

CAUSING DEATH v. SHORTENING LIFE: As was discussed at length in the previous chapter concerning the 1997 Supreme Court case of Washington v. Glucksberg, the single most difficult concept is resolving the elusive distinction between medication that causes death or merely shortens life.

Consider the rule of law that holds that killing an individual is murder regardless of how much time is taken from the victim. Killing a felon on his way to the gallows is murder, no less than if the victim was in the prime of live. Thus, the rule is that shortening a life, even by minutes, is still murder. But, medication that relieves pain with the concomitant shortening of the patient's life is deemed a valid medical practice.

The court in <u>Gonzales</u>, considered this distinction with the following observation:

> The Government contends the Attorney General's decision here is a legal, not a medical, one. This generality, however, does not suffice. The Attorney General's Interpretive Rule, and the Office of Legal Counsel memo it incorporates, place extensive reliance on medical judgments and the views of the medical community in concluding that assisted suicide is not a "legitimate medical purpose." [citation omitted] (noting the <u>"medical" distinctions between assisting suicide and giving sufficient medication to alleviate pain</u>. [citation omitted]
>
> [<u>Gonzales</u> at 267 (emphasis supplied)]

The government tried to deal with this distinction as follows:

> A prescription, the Government argues, necessarily implies that the substance is being made available to a patient for a legitimate medical purpose. The statute, in this view, requires an anterior judgment about the term "medical" or "medicine." The Government contends ordinary usage of these words ineluctably refers to a healing or curative art, which by these terms cannot embrace the intentional hastening of a patient's death.
>
> [<u>Gonzales</u> at 272]

<u>OREGON LAW UPHELD</u>: The crux of the Supreme Court's decision in <u>Gonzales</u> can be found in the following succinct statements dealing with the patient seeking physician-assisted suicide, the physician administering to the patient, and the supremacy of state law—in this case that of the State of Oregon in its Death with Dignity Act.

> The Attorney General … is not authorized to make a rule declaring illegitimate a <u>medical standard for care and treatment of patients</u> that is **specifically authorized under state law**.

....

> The Interpretive Rule thus purports to declare that using controlled substances for physician-assisted suicide is a crime, an authority that goes well beyond the Attorney General's statutory power to register or deregister.

> [Gonzales at 258, 261 (emphasis supplied)]

DISSENTING OPINIONS

Justice Scalia filed a dissenting opinion which was joined by Chief Justice Roberts and Justice Thomas. Justice Thomas also filed a separate dissent. Thus, Gonzales was a case decided by a divided court 6:3.

The core argument in these dissenting opinions was that physician-assisted suicide is not the practice of medicine. Accordingly, the physicians so employed should lose their license to prescribe controlled substances, which would virtually put these physicians out of business.

DEFINITION OF MEDICINE: To structure his point, Justice Scalia in his dissenting opinion quotes from Webster's dictionary concerning the definition of "medicine" and then looks to the American Medical Association for its position on physician-assisted suicide.

> See Webster's New International Dictionary 1954 (2d ed. 1950) (hereinafter Webster's Second) (defining "prescription" as "[a] written direction for the preparation and use of a *medicine*"); *id.,* at 1527 (**defining "medicine"** as "[a]ny substance or preparation used in *treating disease*")

> [Gonzales at 278 (emphasis supplied)]

> [V]irtually every medical authority from Hippocrates to the current American Medical Association (AMA) confirms that assisting suicide has seldom or never been viewed as a form of "prevention, cure, or alleviation of disease," and (even more so) that assisting suicide is not

a "legitimate" branch of that "science and art." [citation omitted] **Indeed, the AMA has determined that "'[p]hysician-assisted suicide is fundamentally incompatible with the physician's role as healer.'"** *Washington* v. *Glucksberg,* 521 U.S. 702, 731 (1997). "[T]he overwhelming weight of authority in judicial decisions, the past and present policies of nearly all of the States and of the Federal Government, and the clear, firm and unequivocal views of the leading associations within the American medical and nursing professions, establish that <u>assisting in suicide . . . is not a legitimate medical purpose.</u>" OLC Memo, *supra,* at 129a. See also *Glucksberg, supra,* at 710, n. 8 <u>(prohibitions or condemnations of assisted suicide in 50 jurisdictions, including 47 States, the District of Columbia, and 2 Territories).</u>

[<u>Gonzales</u> at 286 (emphasis supplied]

EUGENIC INFANTICIDE: Justice Scalia continues his dissent by comparing the "legitimacy of physician-assisted suicide" with "eugenic infanticide," while finding a place to quote "intelligent design":

It is, in other words, perfectly consistent with an **intelligent "design** of the statute" to give the Nation's chief law enforcement official, not its chief health official, broad discretion over the substantive standards that govern registration and deregistration. That is *especially* true where the contested "scientific and medical" judgment at issue has to do with <u>the legitimacy of physician-assisted suicide,</u> which <u>ultimately rests, not on "science" or "medicine," but on a naked value judgment.</u> It no more depends upon a "quintessentially medical judgmen[t]," *ante,* at 267, than does the legitimacy of polygamy or **eugenic infanticide.** And it requires no particular *medical* training to undertake the objective inquiry into how the continuing traditions of Western medicine have consistently treated this subject.

[citation omitted] The Secretary's supposedly superior "medical expertise" to make "medical judgments," *ante,* at 266, is strikingly irrelevant to the case at hand.

[Gonzales at 296 (emphasis supplied)]

50 AMERICAN JURISDICTIONS: Justice Scalia ends his dissent by observing the "condemnation of assisted suicide by 50 American jurisdictions." This does not refer to the 50 states, since Oregon is not a condemning state.

[T]he condemnation of assisted suicide by 50 American jurisdictions supports the Attorney General's view. The Attorney General may therefore weigh a physician's participation in assisted suicide as a factor counseling against his registration, or in favor of deregistration....

[Gonzales at 297]

The Court's decision today is perhaps driven by a feeling that the subject of assisted suicide is none of the Federal Government's business. It is easy to sympathize with that position. The prohibition or deterrence of assisted suicide is certainly not among the enumerated powers conferred on the United States by the Constitution, and it is within the realm of public morality *(bonos mores)* traditionally addressed by the so-called police power of the States.

[Gonzales at 298]

FEDERAL-STATE BALANCE

The conclusion of the majority opinion frames the case as one of states rights:

The Government, in the end, maintains that the prescript-tion requirement delegates to a single <u>executive officer</u> [Attorney General Ashcroft] the <u>power to effect a radical shift of authority from the States to the Federal Government</u> to define general standards of medical practice in every locality. The text and structure of the CSA show that Congress did not have this far-reaching intent to alter the **<u>federal-state balance</u>** and the congressional role in maintaining it.

[<u>Gonzales</u> at 275 (emphasis supplied)]

FRIEND OF THE COURT BRIEFS: <u>Gonzales</u> was extremely

controversial, both: a) as to the lightning subjects of physician-assisted suicide and the Oregon Death with Dignity Act, and b) as to the issue of federal-state balance.

Amici curiae briefs were submitted by many interested parties. Briefs in favor of maintaining the Attorney General's executive power as exercised in an attempt to overturn the Oregon Death with Dignity Act included:

> American Center for Law and Justice
> Americans United for Life
> Catholic Medical Association
> Christian Medical Association
> Focus on the Family
> International Task Force on Euthanasia and Assisted Suicide
> National Association of Pro-Life Nurses
> National Legal Center for the Medically Dependent & Disabled
> Not Dead Yet
> Pro-Life Legal Defense Fund
> Thomas More Society
> United States Conference of Catholic Bishops
> Senator Rick Santorum

Briefs against maintaining the Attorney General's executive power as exercised in an attempt to overturn the Oregon Death with Dignity Act included:

> California
> District of Columbia
> Mississippi
> Missouri
> Montana
> American Civil Liberties Union
> American College of Legal Medicine
> American Public Health Association

Autonomy, Inc
Cato Institute
Coalition of Medical Associations and Societies
Coalition of Mental Health Professionals
Healthlaw Professors
Members of the Oregon Congressional Delegation
Margaret P. Battin
Richard Briffault
Religious and Religious Freedom Organizations and Leaders

Additional briefs were filed by: Physicians for Compassionate Care Educational Foundation, and Surviving Family Members.

CONCLUSION

The 2006 Supreme Court decision in Gonzales v. Oregon can, on the one hand, be narrowly construed as a case simply enjoining an "interpretive rule" of the Attorney General which interpreted the federal Control Substance Act as banning the use of lethal does of medication to end patients' lives with dignity.

On the other hand, the decision can and should be broadly interpreted as forbidding the federal executive branch from interfering with state Death with Dignity Acts.

At the end, after all the court decisions and opinions were finished, the Oregon Death with Dignity Act remained in full force and effect.

Appendix-A
Oregon Death With Dignity Act (2009)

Chapter 127 — Powers of Attorney; Advance Directives for Health Care; Physician Orders for Life-Sustaining Treatment Registry; Declarations for Mental Health Treatment; Death with Dignity

2009 EDITION
THE OREGON DEATH WITH DIGNITY ACT

Section 1
General Provisions

Note: The division headings, subdivision headings and leadlines for 127.800 to 127.890, 127.895 and 127.897 were enacted as part of Ballot Measure 16 (1994) and were not provided by Legislative Counsel.

127.800 §1.01. Definitions. The following words and phrases, whenever used in ORS 127.800 to 127.897, have the following meanings:

(1) **"Adult"** means an individual who is 18 years of age or older.

(2) **"Attending physician"** means the physician who has primary responsibility for the care of the patient and treatment of the patient's terminal disease.

(3) **"Capable"** means that in the opinion of a court or in the opinion of the patient's attending physician or consulting physician, psychiatrist or psychologist, a patient has the ability to make and communicate health care decisions to health care providers, including communication through persons familiar with the patient's manner of communicating if those persons are available.

(4) **"Consulting physician"** means a physician who is qualified by specialty or experience to make a professional diagnosis and prognosis regarding the patient's disease.

page-A1

(5) **"Counseling"** means one or more consultations as necessary between a state licensed psychiatrist or psychologist and a patient for the purpose of determining that the patient is capable and not suffering from a psychiatric or psychological disorder or depression causing impaired judgment.

(6) **"Health care provider"** means a person licensed, certified or otherwise authorized or permitted by the law of this state to administer health care or dispense medication in the ordinary course of business or practice of a profession, and includes a health care facility.

(7) **"Informed decision"** means a decision by a qualified patient, to request and obtain a prescription to end his or her life in a humane and dignified manner, that is based on an appreciation of the relevant facts and after being fully informed by the attending physician of: (a) His or her medical diagnosis; (b) His or her prognosis; (c) The potential risks associated with taking the medication to be prescribed; (d) The probable result of taking the medication to be prescribed; and (e) The feasible alternatives, including, but not limited to, comfort care, hospice care and pain control.

(8) **"Medically confirmed"** means the medical opinion of the attending physician has been confirmed by a consulting physician who has examined the patient and the patient's relevant medical records.

(9) **"Patient"** means a person who is under the care of a physician.

(10) **"Physician"** means a doctor of medicine or osteopathy licensed to practice medicine by the Oregon Medical Board.

(11) **"Qualified patient"** means a capable adult who is a resident of Oregon and has satisfied the requirements of ORS 127.800 to 127.897 in order to obtain a prescription for medication to end his or her life in a humane and dignified manner.

(12) **"Terminal disease"** means an incurable and irreversible disease that has been medically confirmed and will, within reasonable medical judgment, produce death within six months. [1995 c.3 §1.01; 1999 c.423 §1]

Section 2
Written Request for Medication to End One's Life in a Humane and Dignified Manner

127.805 §2.01. Who may initiate a written request for medication.

(1) An adult who is capable, is a resident of Oregon, and has been determined by the attending physician and consulting physician to be suffering from a terminal disease, and who has voluntarily expressed his or her wish to die, may make a written request for medication for the purpose of ending his or her life in a humane and dignified manner in accordance with ORS 127.800 to 127.897.

(2) No person shall qualify under the provisions of ORS 127.800 to 127.897 solely because of age or disability. [1995 c.3 §2.01; 1999 c.423 §2]

127.810 §2.02. Form of the written request.

(1) A valid request for medication under ORS 127.800 to 127.897 shall be in substantially the form described in ORS 127.897, signed and dated by the patient and witnessed by at least two individuals who, in the presence of the patient, attest that to the best of their knowledge and belief the patient is capable, acting voluntarily, and is not being coerced to sign the request.

(2) One of the witnesses shall be a person who is not: (a) A relative of the patient by blood, marriage or adoption; (b) A person who at the time the request is signed would be entitled to any portion of the estate of the qualified patient upon death under any will or by operation of law; or (c) An owner, operator or employee

of a health care facility where the qualified patient is receiving medical treatment or is a resident.

(3) The patient's attending physician at the time the request is signed shall not be a witness.

(4) If the patient is a patient in a long term care facility at the time the written request is made, one of the witnesses shall be an individual designated by the facility and having the qualifications specified by the Department of Human Services by rule. [1995 c.3 §2.02]

(Safeguards)

Section 3
127.815 §3.01. Attending physician responsibilities.

(1) The attending physician shall: (a) Make the initial determination of whether a patient has a terminal disease, is capable, and has made the request voluntarily; (b) Request that the patient demonstrate Oregon residency pursuant to ORS 127.860; (c) To ensure that the patient is making an informed decision, inform the patient of: (A) His or her medical diagnosis; (B) His or her prognosis; (C) The potential risks associated with taking the medication to be prescribed; (D) The probable result of taking the medication to be prescribed; and (E) The feasible alternatives, including, but not limited to, comfort care, hospice care and pain control; (d) Refer the patient to a consulting physician for medical confirmation of the diagnosis, and for a determination that the patient is capable and acting voluntarily; (e) Refer the patient for counseling if appropriate pursuant to ORS 127.825; (f) Recommend that the patient notify next of kin; (g) Counsel the patient about the importance of having another person present when the patient takes the medication prescribed pursuant to ORS 127.800 to 127.897 and of not taking the medication in a public place; (h) Inform the patient that he or she has an opportunity to rescind the request at any time and in any manner, and offer the

patient an opportunity to rescind at the end of the 15 day waiting period pursuant to ORS 127.840; (i) Verify, immediately prior to writing the prescription for medication under ORS 127.800 to 127.897, that the patient is making an informed decision; (j) Fulfill the medical record documentation requirements of ORS 127.855; (k) Ensure that all appropriate steps are carried out in accordance with ORS 127.800 to 127.897 prior to writing a prescription for medication to enable a qualified patient to end his or her life in a humane and dignified manner; and (L) (A) Dispense medications directly, including ancillary medications intended to facilitate the desired effect to minimize the patient's discomfort, provided the attending physician is registered as a dispensing physician with the Oregon Medical Board, has a current Drug Enforcement Administration certificate and complies with any applicable administrative rule; or (B) With the patient's written consent: (i) Contact a pharmacist and inform the pharmacist of the prescription; and (ii) Deliver the written prescription [sic] personally or by mail to the pharmacist, who will dispense the medications to either the patient, the attending physician or an expressly identified agent of the patient. (2) Notwithstanding any other provision of law, the attending physician may sign the patient's death certificate. [1995 c.3 §3.01; 1999 c.423 §3]

127.820 §3.02. Consulting physician confirmation.

Before a patient is qualified under ORS 127.800 to 127.897, a consulting physician shall examine the patient and his or her relevant medical records and confirm, in writing, the attending physician's diagnosis that the patient is suffering from a terminal disease, and verify that the patient is capable, is acting voluntarily and has made an informed decision. [1995 c.3 §3.02]

127.825 §3.03. Counseling referral.

If in the opinion of the attending physician or the consulting physician a patient may be suffering from a psychiatric or psychological disorder or depression causing impaired judgment, either physician shall refer the patient for counseling. No medication to end a patient's life in a humane and dignified manner shall be prescribed until the person performing the counseling determines that the patient is not suffering from a psychiatric or psychological disorder or depression causing impaired judgment. [1995 c.3 §3.03; 1999 c.423 §4]

127.830 §3.04. Informed decision.

No person shall receive a prescription for medication to end his or her life in a humane and dignified manner unless he or she has made an informed decision as defined in ORS 127.800 (7). Immediately prior to writing a prescription for medication under ORS 127.800 to 127.897, the attending physician shall verify that the patient is making an informed decision. [1995 c.3 §3.04]

127.835 §3.05. Family notification.

The attending physician shall recommend that the patient notify the next of kin of his or her request for medication pursuant to ORS 127.800 to 127.897. A patient who declines or is unable to notify next of kin shall not have his or her request denied for that reason. [1995 c.3 §3.05; 1999 c.423 §6]

127.840 §3.06. Written and oral requests.

In order to receive a prescription for medication to end his or her life in a humane and dignified manner, a qualified patient shall have made an oral request and a written request, and reiterate the oral request to his or her attending physician no less than fifteen

(15) days after making the initial oral request. At the time the qualified patient makes his or her second oral request, the attending physician shall offer the patient an opportunity to rescind the request. [1995 c.3 §3.06]

127.845 §3.07. Right to rescind request.

A patient may rescind his or her request at any time and in any manner without regard to his or her mental state. No prescription for medication under ORS 127.800 to 127.897 may be written without the attending physician offering the qualified patient an opportunity to rescind the request. [1995 c.3 §3.07]

127.850 §3.08. Waiting periods.

No less than fifteen (15) days shall elapse between the patient's initial oral request and the writing of a prescripttion under ORS 127.800 to 127.897. No less than 48 hours shall elapse between the patient's written request and the writing of a prescription under ORS 127.800 to 127.897. [1995 c.3 §3.08]

127.855 §3.09. Medical record documentation requirements.

The following shall be documented or filed in the patient's medical record:

(1) All oral requests by a patient for medication to end his or her life in a humane and dignified manner;

(2) All written requests by a patient for medication to end his or her life in a humane and dignified manner;

(3) The attending physician's diagnosis and prognosis, determination that the patient is capable, acting voluntarily and has made an informed decision;

(4) The consulting physician's diagnosis and prognosis, and verification that the patient is capable, acting voluntarily and has made an informed decision;

(5) A report of the outcome and determinations made during counseling, if performed;

(6) The attending physician's offer to the patient to rescind his or her request at the time of the patient's second oral request pursuant to ORS 127.840; and

(7) A note by the attending physician indicating that all requirements under ORS 127.800 to 127.897 have been met and indicating the steps taken to carry out the request, including a notation of the medication prescribed. [1995 c.3 §3.09]

127.860 §3.10. Residency requirement.

Only requests made by Oregon residents under ORS 127.800 to 127.897 shall be granted. Factors demonstrating Oregon residency include but are not limited to:

(1) Possession of an Oregon driver license;

(2) Registration to vote in Oregon;

(3) Evidence that the person owns or leases property in Oregon; or

(4) Filing of an Oregon tax return for the most recent tax year. [1995 c.3 §3.10; 1999 c.423 §8]

127.865 §3.11. Reporting requirements.

(1)(a) The Oregon Health Authority shall annually review a sample of records maintained pursuant to ORS 127.800 to 127.897. (b) The authority shall require any health care provider upon dispensing medication pursuant to ORS 127.800 to 127.897 to file a copy of the dispensing record with the authority.

(2) The authority shall make rules to facilitate the collection of information regarding compliance with ORS 127.800 to 127.897. Except as otherwise required by law, the information collected shall not be a public record and may not be made available for inspection by the public.

(3) The authority shall generate and make available to the public an annual statistical report of information collected under subsection (2) of this section. [1995 c.3 §3.11; 1999 c.423 §9; 2001 c.104 §40; 2009 c.595 §89]

127.870 §3.12. Effect on construction of wills, contracts and statutes.

(1) No provision in a contract, will or other agreement, whether written or oral, to the extent the provision would affect whether a person may make or rescind a request for medication to end his or her life in a humane and dignified manner, shall be valid.

(2) No obligation owing under any currently existing contract shall be conditioned or affected by the making or rescinding of a request, by a person, for medication to end his or her life in a humane and dignified manner. [1995 c.3 §3.12]

127.875 §3.13. Insurance or annuity policies.

The sale, procurement, or issuance of any life, health, or accident insurance or annuity policy or the rate charged for any policy shall not be conditioned upon or affected by the making or rescinding of a request, by a person, for medication to end his or her life in a humane and dignified manner. Neither shall a qualified patient's act of ingesting medication to end his or her life in a humane and dignified manner have an effect upon a life, health, or accident insurance or annuity policy. [1995 c.3 §3.13]

127.880 §3.14. Construction of Act.

Nothing in ORS 127.800 to 127.897 shall be construed to authorize a physician or any other person to end a patient's life by lethal injection, mercy killing or active euthanasia. Actions taken in accordance with ORS 127.800 to 127.897 shall not, for any purpose, constitute suicide, assisted suicide, mercy killing or homicide, under the law. [1995 c.3 §3.14]

Section 4
Immunities and Liabilities

127.885 §4.01. Immunities; basis for prohibiting health care provider from participation; notification; permissible sanctions.

Except as provided in ORS 127.890:

(1) No person shall be subject to civil or criminal liability or professional disciplinary action for participating in good faith compliance with ORS 127.800 to 127.897. This includes being present when a qualified patient takes the prescribed medication to end his or her life in a humane and dignified manner.

(2) No professional organization or association, or health care provider, may subject a person to censure, discipline, suspension, loss of license, loss of privileges, loss of membership or other penalty for participating or refusing to participate in good faith compliance with ORS 127.800 to 127.897.

(3) No request by a patient for or provision by an attending physician of medication in good faith compliance with the provisions of ORS 127.800 to 127.897 shall constitute neglect for any purpose of law or provide the sole basis for the appointment of a guardian or conservator.

(4) No health care provider shall be under any duty, whether by contract, by statute or by any other legal requirement to participate in the provision to a qualified patient of medication to end his or her life in a humane and dignified manner. If a health care provider is unable or unwilling to carry out a patient's request under ORS 127.800 to 127.897, and the patient transfers his or her care to a new health care provider, the prior health care provider shall transfer, upon request, a copy of the patient's relevant medical records to the new health care provider.

(5)(a) Notwithstanding any other provision of law, a health care provider may prohibit another health care provider from participating in ORS 127.800 to 127.897 on the premises of the prohibiting provider if the prohibiting provider has notified the health care provider of the prohibiting provider's policy regarding participating in ORS 127.800 to 127.897. Nothing in this paragraph prevents a health care provider from providing health care services to a patient that do not constitute participation in ORS 127.800 to 127.897.

(b) Notwithstanding the provisions of subsections (1) to (4) of this section, a health care provider may subject another health care provider to the sanctions stated in this paragraph if the sanctioning health care provider has notified the sanctioned provider prior to participation in ORS 127.800 to 127.897 that it prohibits participation in ORS 127.800 to 127.897:

(A) Loss of privileges, loss of membership or other sanction provided pursuant to the medical staff bylaws, policies and procedures of the sanctioning health care provider if the sanctioned provider is a member of the sanctioning provider's medical staff and participates in ORS 127.800 to 127.897 while on the health care facility premises, as defined in ORS 442.015, of the sanctioning health care provider, but not including the private medical office of a physician or other provider;

(B) Termination of lease or other property contract or other nonmonetary remedies provided by lease contract, not including loss or restriction of medical staff privileges or exclusion from a provider panel, if the sanctioned provider participates in ORS 127.800 to 127.897 while on the premises of the sanctioning health care provider or on property that is owned by or under the direct control of the sanctioning health care provider; or

(C) Termination of contract or other nonmonetary remedies provided by contract if the sanctioned provider participates in ORS 127.800 to 127.897 while acting in the course and scope of the sanctioned provider's capacity as an employee or independent contractor of the sanctioning health care provider. Nothing in this subparagraph shall be construed to prevent:

(i) A health care provider from participating in ORS 127.800 to 127.897 while acting outside the course and scope of the provider's capacity as an employee or independent contractor; or

(ii) A patient from contracting with his or her attending physician and consulting physician to act outside the course and scope of the provider's capacity as an employee or independent contractor of the sanctioning health care provider.

(c) A health care provider that imposes sanctions pursuant to paragraph (b) of this subsection must follow all due process and other procedures the sanctioning health care provider may have that are related to the imposition of sanctions on another health care provider.

(d) For purposes of this subsection:

(A) "Notify" means a separate statement in writing to the health care provider specifically informing the health care provider prior to the provider's participation in ORS 127.800 to 127.897 of the sanctioning health care provider's policy about participation in activities covered by ORS 127.800 to 127.897.

(B) "Participate in ORS 127.800 to 127.897" means to perform the duties of an attending physician pursuant to ORS 127.815, the consulting physician function pursuant to ORS 127.820 or the counseling function pursuant to ORS 127.825. "Participate in ORS 127.800 to 127.897" does not include:

(i) Making an initial determination that a patient has a terminal disease and informing the patient of the medical prognosis;

(ii) Providing information about the Oregon Death with Dignity Act to a patient upon the request of the patient;

(iii) Providing a patient, upon the request of the patient, with a referral to another physician; or

(iv) A patient contracting with his or her attending physician and consulting physician to act outside of the course and scope of the provider's capacity as an employee or independent contractor of the sanctioning health care provider.

(6) Suspension or termination of staff membership or privileges under subsection (5) of this section is not reportable under ORS 441.820. Action taken pursuant to ORS 127.810, 127.815, 127.820 or 127.825 shall not be the sole basis for a report of unprofessional or dishonorable conduct under ORS 677.415 (3), (4), (5) or (6).

(7) No provision of ORS 127.800 to 127.897 shall be construed to allow a lower standard of care for patients in the community where the patient is treated or a similar community. [1995 c.3 §4.01; 1999 c.423 §10; 2003 c.554 §3]

Note: As originally enacted by the people, the leadline to section 4.01 read "Immunities." The remainder of the leadline was added by editorial action.

127.890 §4.02. Liabilities.

(1) A person who without authorization of the patient willfully alters or forges a request for medication or conceals or destroys a rescission of that request with the intent or effect of causing the patient's death shall be guilty of a Class A felony.

(2) A person who coerces or exerts undue influence on a patient to request medication for the purpose of ending the patient's life, or to destroy a rescission of such a request, shall be guilty of a Class A felony.

(3) Nothing in ORS 127.800 to 127.897 limits further liability for civil damages resulting from other negligent conduct or intentional misconduct by any person.

(4) The penalties in ORS 127.800 to 127.897 do not preclude criminal penalties applicable under other law for conduct which is

inconsistent with the provisions of ORS 127.800 to 127.897. [1995 c.3 §4.02]

127.892 Claims by governmental entity for costs incurred.

Any governmental entity that incurs costs resulting from a person terminating his or her life pursuant to the provisions of ORS 127.800 to 127.897 in a public place shall have a claim against the estate of the person to recover such costs and reasonable attorney fees related to enforcing the claim. [1999 c.423 §5a]

Section 5
Severability

127.895 §5.01. Severability.

Any section of ORS 127.800 to 127.897 being held invalid as to any person or circumstance shall not affect the application of any other section of ORS 127.800 to 127.897 which can be given full effect without the invalid section or application. [1995 c.3 §5.01]

Section 6
Form of the Request

127.897 §6.01. Form of the request.

A request for a medication as authorized by ORS 127.800 to 127.897 shall be in substantially the following form:

REQUEST FOR MEDICATION
TO END MY LIFE IN A HUMANE
AND DIGNIFIED MANNER

I, _____, am an adult of sound mind.

I am suffering from _____, which my attending physician has determined is a terminal disease and which has been medically confirmed by a consulting physician.

I have been fully informed of my diagnosis, prognosis, the nature of medication to be prescribed and potential associated risks, the expected result, and the feasible alternatives, including comfort care, hospice care and pain control.

I request that my attending physician prescribe medication that will end my life in a humane and dignified manner.

INITIAL ONE:

_____ I have informed my family of my decision and taken their opinions into consideration.

_____ I have decided not to inform my family of my decision.

_____ I have no family to inform of my decision.

I understand that I have the right to rescind this request at any time.

I understand the full import of this request and I expect to die when I take the medication to be prescribed. I further understand that although most deaths occur within three hours, my death may take longer and my physician has counseled me about this possibility.

I make this request voluntarily and without reservation, and I accept full moral responsibility for my actions.

Signed: _____

Dated: _____

DECLARATION OF WITNESSES

We declare that the person signing this request:

(a) Is personally known to us or has provided proof of identity;

(b) Signed this request in our presence;

(c) Appears to be of sound mind and not under duress, fraud or undue influence;

(d) Is not a patient for whom either of us is attending physician.

_____Witness 1/Date
_____Witness 2/Date

NOTE: One witness shall not be a relative (by blood, marriage or adoption) of the person signing this request, shall not be entitled to any portion of the person's estate upon death and shall not own, operate or be employed at a health care facility where the person is a patient or resident. If the patient is an inpatient at a health care facility, one of the witnesses shall be an individual designated by the facility.
[1995 c.3 §6.01; 1999 c.423 §11]

PENALTIES

127.990 [Formerly part of 97.990; repealed by 1993 c.767 §29]

127.995 Penalties.

(1) It shall be a Class A felony for a person without authorization of the principal to willfully alter, forge, conceal or destroy an instrument, the reinstatement or revocation of an instrument or any other evidence or document reflecting the principal's desires and interests, with the intent and effect of causing a withholding or withdrawal of lifesustaining procedures or of artificially administered nutrition and hydration which hastens the death of the principal.

(2) Except as provided in subsection (1) of this section, it shall be a Class A misdemeanor for a person without authorization of the principal to willfully alter, forge, conceal or destroy an instrument, the reinstatement or revocation of an instrument, or any other evidence or document reflecting the principal's desires and interests with the intent or effect of affecting a health care decision. [Formerly 127.585]

State of Oregon, Oregon Health Authority:
http://public.health.oregon.gov/ProviderPartnerResources/EvaluationResearch/DeathwithDignityAct/Pages/index.aspx

The Oregon Death with Dignity Act:
A Guidebook for Health Care Professionals

http://www.ohsu.edu/xd/education/continuing-education/center-for-ethics/ethics-outreach/upload/Oregon-Death-with-Dignity-Act-Guidebook.pdf

1. *Purpose of the Guidebook*
Patrick Dunn, M.D.
2. *The Meaning Behind the Patient's Request*
Terri Schmidt, M.D.
3. *Conscientious Practice*
Bonnie Reagan, M.D., R.N.
4. *Hospice, Palliative Care, and Comfort Care*
Deborah Whiting Jaques, R.T. (R)(ARRT), Ann Jackson, M.B.A.
5. *Patient Rights and Responsibilities*
(Rev.) John F. Tuohey, Ph.D.
6. *Family Needs and Concerns*
Susan Hedlund, M.S.W., L.C.S.W., Bonnie Reagan, M.D., R.N.
7. *Attending Physician and Consulting Physician*
Patrick Dunn, M.D., Bonnie Reagan, M.D., R.N.
8. *The Role of Other Health Care Professionals*
Pamela J. Miller, M.S.W., Ph.D.
9. *Mental Health Consultation*
Elizabeth Goy, Ph.D., Linda Ganzini, M.D., Tony Farrenkopf, Ph.D.
10. *Pharmacists and Pharmacy-Related Issues*
Gary Schnabel, R.N., R.Ph., Joseph Schnabel, Pharm.D., R.Ph.
11. *Emergency Department and Emergency Medical Services*
Terri Schmidt, M.D.
12. *Responding to Professional Non-Compliance*
Kathleen Haley, J.D., Susan W. Tolle, M.D.
13. *Financial Issues*
Gwen Dayton, J.D.
14. *Oregon Department of Human Services Reporting*
Katrina Hedberg, M.D., M.P.H.
15. *Liability and Negligence*
Kelly Hagan, J.D.

[page left blank]

[2009 EDITION]
[THE WASHINGTON DEATH WITH DIGNITY ACT]

RCW 70.245.010 Definitions.

The definitions in this section apply throughout this chapter unless the context clearly requires otherwise.

(1) **"Adult"** means an individual who is eighteen years of age or older.

(2) **"Attending physician"** means the physician who has primary responsibility for the care of the patient and treatment of the patient's terminal disease.

(3) **"Competent"** means that, in the opinion of a court or in the opinion of the patient's attending physician or consulting physician, psychiatrist, or psychologist, a patient has the ability to make and communicate an informed decision to health care providers, including communication through persons familiar with the patient's manner of communicating if those persons are available.

(4) **"Consulting physician"** means a physician who is qualified by specialty or experience to make a professional diagnosis and prognosis regarding the patient's disease.

(5) **"Counseling"** means one or more consultations as necessary between a state licensed psychiatrist or psychologist and a patient for the purpose of determining that the patient is competent and not suffering from a psychiatric or psychological disorder or depression causing impaired judgment.

(6) **"Health care provider"** means a person licensed, certified, or otherwise authorized or permitted by law to administer health care or dispense medication in the ordinary course of business or practice of a profession, and includes a health care facility.

(7) **"Informed decision"** means a decision by a qualified patient, to request and obtain a prescription for medication that the qualified patient may self-administer to end his or her life in a

humane and dignified manner, that is based on an appreciation of the relevant facts and after being fully informed by the attending physician of:

(a) His or her medical diagnosis;

(b) His or her prognosis;

(c) The potential risks associated with taking the medication to be prescribed;

(d) The probable result of taking the medication to be prescribed; and

(e) The feasible alternatives including, but not limited to, comfort care, hospice care, and pain control.

(8) **"Medically confirmed"** means the medical opinion of the attending physician has been confirmed by a consulting physician who has examined the patient and the patient's relevant medical records.

(9) **"Patient"** means a person who is under the care of a physician.

(10) **"Physician"** means a doctor of medicine or osteopathy licensed to practice medicine in the state of Washington.

(11) **"Qualified patient"** means a competent adult who is a resident of Washington state and has satisfied the requirements of this chapter in order to obtain a prescription for medication that the qualified patient may self-administer to end his or her life in a humane and dignified manner.

(12) **"Self-administer"** means a qualified patient's act of ingesting medication to end his or her life in a humane and dignified manner.

(13) **"Terminal disease"** means an incurable and irreversible disease that has been medically confirmed and will, within reasonable medical judgment, produce death within six months.

[2009 c 1 § 1 (Initiative Measure No. 1000, approved November 4, 2008).]

RCW 70.245.020 Written request for medication.

(1) An adult who is competent, is a resident of Washington state, and has been determined by the attending physician and consulting physician to be suffering from a terminal disease, and who has voluntarily expressed his or her wish to die, may make a written request for medication that the patient may self-administer to end his or her life in a humane and dignified manner in accordance with this chapter.

(2) A person does not qualify under this chapter solely because of age or disability.

[2009 c 1 § 2 (Initiative Measure No. 1000, approved November 4, 2008).]

RCW 70.245.030 Form of the written request.

(1) A valid request for medication under this chapter shall be in substantially the form described in RCW 70.245.220, signed and dated by the patient and witnessed by at least two individuals who, in the presence of the patient, attest that to the best of their knowledge and belief the patient is competent, acting voluntarily, and is not being coerced to sign the request.

(2) One of the witnesses shall be a person who is not:

(a) A relative of the patient by blood, marriage, or adoption;

(b) A person who at the time the request is signed would be entitled to any portion of the estate of the qualified patient upon death under any will or by operation of law; or

(c) An owner, operator, or employee of a health care facility where the qualified patient is receiving medical treatment or is a resident.

(3) The patient's attending physician at the time the request is signed shall not be a witness.

(4) If the patient is a patient in a long-term care facility at the time the written request is made, one of the witnesses shall be an individual designated by the facility and having the qualifications specified by the department of health by rule.

[2009 c 1 § 3 (Initiative Measure No. 1000, approved November 4, 2008).]

RCW 70.245.040 Attending physician responsibilities.

(1) The attending physician shall:

(a) Make the initial determination of whether a patient has a terminal disease, is competent, and has made the request voluntarily;

(b) Request that the patient demonstrate Washington state residency under RCW 70.245.130;

(c) To ensure that the patient is making an informed decision, inform the patient of:

(i) His or her medical diagnosis;

(ii) His or her prognosis;

(iii) The potential risks associated with taking the medication to be prescribed;

(iv) The probable result of taking the medication to be prescribed; and

(v) The feasible alternatives including, but not limited to, comfort care, hospice care, and pain control;

(d) Refer the patient to a consulting physician for medical confirmation of the diagnosis, and for a determination that the patient is competent and acting voluntarily;

(e) Refer the patient for counseling if appropriate under RCW 70.245.060;

(f) Recommend that the patient notify next of kin;

(g) Counsel the patient about the importance of having another person present when the patient takes the medication prescribed under this chapter and of not taking the medication in a public place;

(h) Inform the patient that he or she has an opportunity to rescind the request at any time and in any manner, and offer the patient an opportunity to rescind at the end of the fifteen-day waiting period under RCW 70.245.090;

(i) Verify, immediately before writing the prescription for medication under this chapter, that the patient is making an informed decision;

(j) Fulfill the medical record documentation requirements of RCW 70.245.120;

(k) Ensure that all appropriate steps are carried out in accordance with this chapter before writing a prescription for medication to enable a qualified patient to end his or her life in a humane and dignified manner; and

(l)(i) Dispense medications directly, including ancillary medications intended to facilitate the desired effect to minimize the patient's discomfort, if the attending physician is authorized under statute and rule to dispense and has a current drug enforcement administration certificate; or

(ii) With the patient's written consent:

(A) Contact a pharmacist and inform the pharmacist of the prescription; and

(B) Deliver the written prescription personally, by mail or facsimile to the pharmacist, who will dispense the medications directly to either the patient, the attending physician, or an expressly identified agent of the patient. Medications dispensed pursuant to this subsection shall not be dispensed by mail or other form of courier.

(2) The attending physician may sign the patient's death certificate which shall list the underlying terminal disease as the cause of death.

[2009 c 1 § 4 (Initiative Measure No. 1000, approved November 4, 2008).]

RCW 70.245.050 Consulting physician confirmation.

Before a patient is qualified under this chapter, a consulting physician shall examine the patient and his or her relevant medical records and confirm, in writing, the attending physician's diagnosis that the patient is suffering from a terminal disease, and verify that the patient is competent, is acting voluntarily, and has made an informed decision.

[2009 c 1 § 5 (Initiative Measure No. 1000, approved November 4, 2008).]

RCW 70.245.060 Counseling referral.

If, in the opinion of the attending physician or the consulting physician, a patient may be suffering from a psychiatric or psychological disorder or depression causing impaired judgment, either physician shall refer the patient for counseling. Medication to end a patient's life in a humane and dignified manner shall not be prescribed until the person performing the counseling determines that the patient is not suffering from a psychiatric or psychological disorder or depression causing impaired judgment.

[2009 c 1 § 6 (Initiative Measure No. 1000, approved November 4, 2008).]

RCW 70.245.070 Informed decision.

A person shall not receive a prescription for medication to end his or her life in a humane and dignified manner unless he or she has made an informed decision. Immediately before writing a prescription for medication under this chapter, the attending physician shall verify that the qualified patient is making an informed decision.

[2009 c 1 § 7 (Initiative Measure No. 1000, approved November 4, 2008).]

RCW 70.245.080 Notification of next of kin.

The attending physician shall recommend that the patient notify the next of kin of his or her request for medication under this chapter. A patient who declines or is unable to notify next of kin shall not have his or her request denied for that reason.

[2009 c 1 § 8 (Initiative Measure No. 1000, approved November 4, 2008).]

RCW 70.245.090 Written and oral requests.

To receive a prescription for medication that the qualified patient may self-administer to end his or her life in a humane and dignified manner, a qualified patient shall have made an oral request and a written request, and reiterate the oral request to his or her attending physician at least fifteen days after making the initial oral request. At the time the qualified patient makes his or her second oral request, the attending physician shall offer the qualified patient an opportunity to rescind the request.

[2009 c 1 § 9 (Initiative Measure No. 1000, approved November 4, 2008).]

RCW 70.245.100 Right to rescind request.

A patient may rescind his or her request at any time and in any manner without regard to his or her mental state. No prescription for medication under this chapter may be written without the attending physician offering the qualified patient an opportunity to rescind the request.

[2009 c 1 § 10 (Initiative Measure No. 1000, approved November 4, 2008).]

RCW 70.245.110 Waiting periods.

(1) At least fifteen days shall elapse between the patient's initial oral request and the writing of a prescription under this chapter.

(2) At least forty-eight hours shall elapse between the date the patient signs the written request and the writing of a prescription under this chapter.

[2009 c 1 § 11 (Initiative Measure No. 1000, approved November 4, 2008).]

RCW 70.245.120 Medical record documentation requirements.

The following shall be documented or filed in the patient's medical record:

(1) All oral requests by a patient for medication to end his or her life in a humane and dignified manner;

(2) All written requests by a patient for medication to end his or her life in a humane and dignified manner;

(3) The attending physician's diagnosis and prognosis, and determination that the patient is competent, is acting voluntarily, and has made an informed decision;

(4) The consulting physician's diagnosis and prognosis, and verification that the patient is competent, is acting voluntarily, and has made an informed decision;

(5) A report of the outcome and determinations made during counseling, if performed;

(6) The attending physician's offer to the patient to rescind his or her request at the time of the patient's second oral request under RCW 70.245.090; and

(7) A note by the attending physician indicating that all requirements under this chapter have been met and indicating the steps taken to carry out the request, including a notation of the medication prescribed.

[2009 c 1 § 12 (Initiative Measure No. 1000, approved November 4, 2008).]

RCW 70.245.130 Residency requirement.

Only requests made by Washington state residents under this chapter may be granted. Factors demonstrating Washington state residency include but are not limited to:

(1) Possession of a Washington state driver's license;

(2) Registration to vote in Washington state; or

(3) Evidence that the person owns or leases property in Washington state.

[2009 c 1 § 13 (Initiative Measure No. 1000, approved November 4, 2008).]

RCW 70.245.140 Disposal of unused medications.

Any medication dispensed under this chapter that was not self-administered shall be disposed of by lawful means.

[2009 c 1 § 14 (Initiative Measure No. 1000, approved November 4, 2008).]

RCW 70.245.150 Reporting of information to the department of health — Adoption of rules — Information collected not a public record — Annual statistical report.

(1)(a) The department of health shall annually review all records maintained under this chapter.

(b) The department of health shall require any health care provider upon writing a prescription or dispensing medication under this chapter to file a copy of the dispensing record and such other administratively required documentation with the department. All administratively required documentation shall be mailed or otherwise transmitted as allowed by department of health rule to the department no later than thirty calendar days after the writing of a prescription and dispensing of medication under this chapter, except that all documents required to be filed with the department by the prescribing physician after the death of the patient shall be mailed no later than thirty calendar days after the date of death of the patient. In the event that anyone required under this chapter to report information to the department of health provides an inadequate or incomplete report, the department shall contact the person to request a complete report.

(2) The department of health shall adopt rules to facilitate the collection of information regarding compliance with this chapter. Except as otherwise required by law, the information collected is not a public record and may not be made available for inspection by the public.

(3) The department of health shall generate and make available to the public an annual statistical report of information collected under subsection (2) of this section.

[2009 c 1 § 15 (Initiative Measure No. 1000, approved November 4, 2008).]

RCW 70.245.160 Effect on construction of wills, contracts, and statutes.

(1) Any provision in a contract, will, or other agreement, whether written or oral, to the extent the provision would affect whether a person may make or rescind a request for medication to end his or her life in a humane and dignified manner, is not valid.

(2) Any obligation owing under any currently existing contract shall not be conditioned or affected by the making or rescinding of a request, by a person, for medication to end his or her life in a humane and dignified manner.

[2009 c 1 § 16 (Initiative Measure No. 1000, approved November 4, 2008).]

RCW 70.245.170 Insurance or annuity policies.

The sale, procurement, or issuance of any life, health, or accident insurance or annuity policy or the rate charged for any policy shall not be conditioned upon or affected by the making or rescinding of a request, by a person, for medication that the patient may self-administer to end his or her life in a humane and dignified manner. A qualified patient's act of ingesting medication to end his or her life in a humane and dignified manner shall not have an effect upon a life, health, or accident insurance or annuity policy.

[2009 c 1 § 17 (Initiative Measure No. 1000, approved November 4, 2008).]

RCW 70.245.180 Authority of chapter — References to practices under this chapter — Applicable standard of care.

(1) Nothing in this chapter authorizes a physician or any other person to end a patient's life by lethal injection, mercy killing, or active euthanasia. Actions taken in accordance with this chapter do not, for any purpose, constitute suicide, assisted suicide, mercy killing, or homicide, under the law. State reports shall not refer to practice under this chapter as "suicide" or "assisted suicide." Consistent with RCW 70.245.010 (7), (11), and (12), 70.245.020(1), 70.245.040(1)(k), 70.245.060, 70.245.070 ,

70.245.090, 70.245.120 (1) and (2), 70.245.160 (1) and (2), 70.245.170, 70.245.190(1) (a) and (d), and70.245.200 (2), state reports shall refer to practice under this chapter as obtaining and self-administering life-ending medication.

(2) Nothing contained in this chapter shall be interpreted to lower the applicable standard of care for the attending physician, consulting physician, psychiatrist or psychologist, or other health care provider participating under this chapter.

[2009 c 1 § 18 (Initiative Measure No. 1000, approved November 4, 2008).]

RCW 70.245.190 Immunities — Basis for prohibiting health care provider from participation — Notification — Permissible sanctions.

(1) Except as provided in RCW 70.245.200 and subsection (2) of this section:

(a) A person shall not be subject to civil or criminal liability or professional disciplinary action for participating in good faith compliance with this chapter. This includes being present when a qualified patient takes the prescribed medication to end his or her life in a humane and dignified manner;

(b) A professional organization or association, or health care provider, may not subject a person to censure, discipline, suspension, loss of license, loss of privileges, loss of membership, or other penalty for participating or refusing to participate in good faith compliance with this chapter;

(c) A patient's request for or provision by an attending physician of medication in good faith compliance with this chapter does not constitute neglect for any purpose of law or provide the sole basis for the appointment of a guardian or conservator; and

(d) Only willing health care providers shall participate in the provision to a qualified patient of medication to end his or her life in a humane and dignified manner. If a health care provider is unable or unwilling to carry out a patient's request under this chapter, and the patient transfers his or her care to a new health care provider, the prior health care provider shall transfer, upon request, a copy of the patient's relevant medical records to the new health care provider.

(2)(a) A health care provider may prohibit another health care provider from participating under chapter 1, Laws of 2009 on the premises of the prohibiting provider if the prohibiting provider has given notice to all health care providers with privileges to practice on the premises and to the general public of the prohibiting provider's policy regarding participating under chapter 1, Laws of 2009. This subsection does not prevent a health care provider from providing health care services to a patient that do not constitute participation under chapter 1, Laws of 2009.

(b) A health care provider may subject another health care provider to the sanctions stated in this subsection if the sanctioning health care provider has notified the sanctioned provider before participation in chapter 1, Laws of 2009 that it prohibits participation in chapter 1, Laws of 2009:

(i) Loss of privileges, loss of membership, or other sanctions provided under the medical staff bylaws, policies, and procedures of the sanctioning health care provider if the sanctioned provider is a member of the sanctioning provider's medical staff and participates in chapter 1, Laws of 2009 while on the health care facility premises of the sanctioning health care provider, but not including the private medical office of a physician or other provider;

(ii) Termination of a lease or other property contract or other nonmonetary remedies provided by a lease contract, not including loss or restriction of medical staff privileges or exclusion from a provider panel, if the sanctioned provider participates in chapter 1, Laws of 2009 while on the premises of the sanctioning health care provider or on property that is owned by or under the direct control of the sanctioning health care provider; or

(iii) Termination of a contract or other nonmonetary remedies provided by contract if the sanctioned provider participates in chapter 1, Laws of 2009 while acting in the course and scope of the sanctioned provider's capacity as an employee or independent contractor of the sanctioning health care provider. Nothing in this subsection (2)(b)(iii) prevents:

(A) A health care provider from participating in chapter 1, Laws of 2009 while acting outside the course and scope of the provider's capacity as an employee or independent contractor; or

(B) A patient from contracting with his or her attending physician and consulting physician to act outside the course and scope of the provider's capacity as an employee or independent contractor of the sanctioning health care provider.

(c) A health care provider that imposes sanctions under (b) of this subsection shall follow all due process and other procedures the sanctioning health care provider may have that are related to the imposition of sanctions on another health care provider.

(d) For the purposes of this subsection:

(i) "Notify" means a separate statement in writing to the health care provider specifically informing the health care provider before the provider's participation in chapter 1, Laws of 2009 of the sanctioning health care provider's policy about participation in activities covered by this chapter.

(ii) "Participate in chapter 1, Laws of 2009" means to perform the duties of an attending physician under RCW 70.245.040, the consulting physician function under RCW 70.245.050, or the counseling function under RCW 70.245.060. "Participate in chapter 1, Laws of 2009" does not include:

(A) Making an initial determination that a patient has a terminal disease and informing the patient of the medical prognosis;

(B) Providing information about the Washington death with dignity act to a patient upon the request of the patient;

(C) Providing a patient, upon the request of the patient, with a referral to another physician; or

(D) A patient contracting with his or her attending physician and consulting physician to act outside of the course and scope of the provider's capacity as an employee or independent contractor of the sanctioning health care provider.

(3) Suspension or termination of staff membership or privileges under subsection (2) of this section is not reportable under RCW 18.130.070. Action taken under RCW 70.245.030, 70.245.040, 70.245.050, or 70.245.060 may not be the sole basis for a report of unprofessional conduct under RCW 18.130.180.

(4) References to "good faith" in subsection (1)(a), (b), and (c) of this section do not allow a lower standard of care for health care providers in the state of Washington.

[2009 c 1 § 19 (Initiative Measure No. 1000, approved November 4, 2008).]

RCW 70.245.200 Willful alteration/forgery — Coercion or undue influence — Penalties — Civil damages — Other penalties not precluded.

(1) A person who without authorization of the patient willfully alters or forges a request for medication or conceals or destroys a rescission of that request with the intent or effect of causing the patient's death is guilty of a class A felony.

(2) A person who coerces or exerts undue influence on a patient to request medication to end the patient's life, or to destroy a rescission of a request, is guilty of a class A felony.

(3) This chapter does not limit further liability for civil damages resulting from other negligent conduct or intentional misconduct by any person.

(4) The penalties in this chapter do not preclude criminal penalties applicable under other law for conduct that is inconsistent with this chapter.

[2009 c 1 § 20 (Initiative Measure No. 1000, approved November 4, 2008).]

RCW 70.245.210 Claims by governmental entity for costs incurred.

Any governmental entity that incurs costs resulting from a person terminating his or her life under this chapter in a public place has a claim against the estate of the person to recover such costs and reasonable attorneys' fees related to enforcing the claim.

[2009 c 1 § 21 (Initiative Measure No. 1000, approved November 4, 2008).]

RCW 70.245.220 Form of the request.

A request for a medication as authorized by this chapter shall be in substantially the following form:

REQUEST FOR MEDICATION TO END MY LIFE IN A HUMAN [HUMANE] AND DIGNIFIED MANNER

I,. . . . . , am an adult of sound mind.

I am suffering from . . . . , which my attending physician has determined is a terminal disease and which has been medically confirmed by a consulting physician.

I have been fully informed of my diagnosis, prognosis, the nature of medication to be prescribed and potential associated risks, the expected result, and the feasible alternatives, including comfort care, hospice care, and pain control.

I request that my attending physician prescribe medication that I may self-administer to end my life in a humane and dignified manner and to contact any pharmacist to fill the prescription.

INITIAL ONE:

. . . . . I have informed my family of my decision and taken their opinions into consideration.

. . . . . I have decided not to inform my family of my decision.

. . . . . I have no family to inform of my decision.

I understand that I have the right to rescind this request at any time.

I understand the full import of this request and I expect to die when I take the medication to be prescribed. I further understand that although most deaths occur within three hours, my death may take longer and my physician has counseled me about this possibility.

I make this request voluntarily and without reservation, and I accept full moral responsibility for my actions.

Signed:. . . . .

Dated:. . . . .

DECLARATION OF WITNESSES

By initialing and signing below on or after the date the person named above signs, we declare that the person making and signing the above request:

Witness 1   Witness 2

Initials   Initials

. . . .   1. Is personally known to us or has
. .   . .   provided proof of identity;
. . . .   2. Signed this request in our presence on
. .   . .   the date of the person's signature;
. . . .   3. Appears to be of sound mind and not
. .   . .   under duress, fraud, or undue influence;
. . . .   4. Is not a patient for whom either of us
. .   . .   is the attending physician.

Printed Name of Witness 1: . . . .

. . .

Signature of Witness 1/Date: . . . .

. . . .

Printed Name of Witness 2: . . . .

. . .

Signature of Witness 2/Date: . . . .

. . . .

NOTE: One witness shall not be a relative by blood, marriage, or adoption of the person signing this request, shall not be entitled to any portion of the person's estate upon death, and shall not own, operate, or be employed at a health care facility where the person is a patient or resident. If the patient is an inpatient at a health care facility, one of the witnesses shall be an individual designated by the facility.

[2009 c 1 § 22 (Initiative Measure No. 1000, approved November 4, 2008).]

RCW 70.245.901 Short title — 2009 c 1 (Initiative Measure No. 1000).

This act may be known and cited as the Washington death with dignity act.

[2009 c 1 § 26 (Initiative Measure No. 1000, approved November 4, 2008).]

RCW 70.245.902 Severability — 2009 c 1 (Initiative Measure No. 1000).

If any provision of this act or its application to any person or circumstance is held invalid, the remainder of the act or the application of the provision to other persons or circumstances is not affected.

[2009 c 1 § 27 (Initiative Measure No. 1000, approved November 4, 2008).]

RCW 70.245.903 Effective dates — 2009 c 1 (Initiative Measure No. 1000).

This act takes effect one hundred twenty days after the election at which it is approved [March 5, 2009], except for section 24 of this act which takes effect July 1, 2009.

[2009 c 1 § 28 (Initiative Measure No. 1000, approved November 4, 2008).]

RCW 70.245.904 Captions, part headings, and subpart headings not law — 2009 c 1 (Initiative Measure No. 1000).

Captions, part headings, and subpart headings used in this act are not any part of the law.

[2009 c 1 § 30 (Initiative Measure No. 1000, approved November 4, 2008).]

WASHINGTON DEATH WITH DIGNITY ACT
http://apps.leg.wa.gov/RCW/default.aspx?cite=70.245

State of Washington, Washington State Department of Health:
http://www.doh.wa.gov/dwda/

NOTES

NOTES

NOTES

NOTES

NOTES

NOTES

www.ingramcontent.com/pod-product-compliance
Lightning Source LLC
Chambersburg PA
CBHW082034190526
45165CB00020B/2502